THE FOCAL EASY GUIDE TO
FINAL CUT PRO X

THE FOCAL EASY GUIDE TO

FINAL CUT PRO X

RICK YOUNG

Focal Press
Taylor & Francis Group

NEW YORK AND LONDON

First published 2013
by Focal Press (Taylor and Francis)
70 Blanchard Road, Suite 402
Burlington, MA 01803

Simultaneously published in the UK
by Focal Press
2 Park Square, Milton Park, Abingdon, Oxon OX14 4RN

Focal Press is an imprint of the Taylor & Francis Group, an informa business

Notices

Knowledge and best practice in this field are constantly changing. As new research and experience broaden our understanding, changes in research methods, professional practices, or medical treatment may become necessary.

Practitioners and researchers must always rely on their own experience and knowledge in evaluating and using any information, methods, compounds, or experiments described herein. In using such information or methods they should be mindful of their own safety and the safety of others, including parties for whom they have a professional responsibility.

Product or corporate names may be trademarks or registered trademarks, and are used only for identification and explanation without intent to infringe.

Library of Congress Cataloging in Publication Data

Application submitted.

ISBN: 978-0-240-52383-5 (pbk)
ISBN: 978-0-240-52385-9 (ebk)

Typeset in Avenir

Project Managed and Typeset by: diacriTech

Printed and bound in the United States of America by Sheridan Books, Inc. (a Sheridan Group company)

Thank you:

Fiona
Ellen
Druman
Ken Stone
Matt Davis
Dennis at Focal
Elizabeth Jolley (for the inspiration)

Contents

Editing 55

Audio 111

Effects   137

Introduction

It was way back in April of 2011 when Apple unveiled Final Cut Pro X to the world. Randy Ubilos, the creator of the original Final Cut Pro, demonstrated the latest version of the software to an excited crowd. The event was the Final Cut Pro User Group NAB SuperMeet. The venue was jam-packed, and Randy's demo was punctuated by cheering and whooping of the crowd as feature after feature was revealed, giving the audience a taste of what was to come.

The aftermath of April 2011 was not so clear-cut. Final Cut Pro X was released in June of 2011. Many in the editing community cried this was no more than a souped-up version of iMovie; others jumped ship to other editors; a few early pioneers seized on the new software, extolling its virtues and looking down the road to a brighter future as the software evolved and developed.

That brighter future has now arrived. I deliberately held off writing the Easy Guide to Final Cut Pro X as certain key features were missing from the original release. Now with many more features and the stability of a later release, Final Cut Pro X is ready for professional work at many levels. The software is fast, streamlined, and effective in delivering edited content. I have used Final Cut Pro X for paying work, on many jobs! With the right person at the controls, the editor is capable of producing results to a high level.

This book is not a "teach you how to do everything book"—this is a "teach you what you need to know; the essentials; how to dive in deep and swim successfully." Consider this book to be a crash course in Final Cut Pro X.

The author demos Final Cut Pro X at
MacVideo Expo, London, Oct. 2011

"Go fly with this software; it's got wings."

Rick Young, May 2012

SYSTEM SETUP

A Word about Preferences

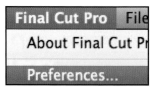

Setting up Preferences is not the most exciting place to start, however, it can save you a lot of hassle later on by getting this right at the start. The Preferences in Final Cut Pro X are relatively sparse compared to the myriad of choices offered in some editing programs.

There are three separate panes: Editing, Playback, and Import.

Editing Preferences

For the most part, the Editing Preferences can be left at their defaults. I suggest activating two options: Show Detailed Trimming Feedback and Position Playhead after Edit Operation.

☑ Show detailed trimming feedback
☑ Position playhead after edit operation

To active Detailed Trimming Feedback means when using the Trim mode while editing, the feedback display will be that of two windows: one showing the outgoing clip and the other showing the incoming clip. You can precisely fine-tune edits by watching the dual display. This functionality will be useful once we begin the editing process.

3

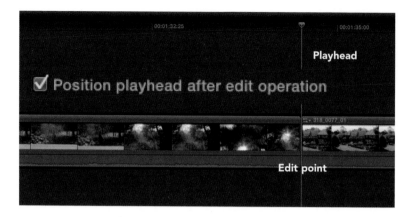

Selecting Position Playhead after Edit Operation means that each time you perform an edit, then what is known as the Playhead, the point which defines where you are in the Timeline, will be left in position immediately after where the edit has taken place.

Playback Preferences

Selecting Position Playhead after Edit Operation means that each time you

As with the Editing Preferences, most of the Playback Preferences can be left at the default settings; however, it is worth understanding the key options in front of you as what you choose will affect the performance of your system. We will work our way down from the top.

Background Render

One of the key features of Final Cut Pro X is Background Rendering.

Rendering: ☑ Background render

This means when you are not working, the computer will render the frames of your movie in full pristine quality for you to view. If you leave Background Rendering switched on, after the defined time (by default 4 seconds), then the computer will kick in and render any media in the Timeline which needs to be processed.

It may be that you don't want the computer to do the rendering while you are working, in which case switch Background

Background render

Render off. Render files consume hard drive space, and while these can be easily deleted, there are times when one may wish to avoid rendering until you are ready.

For the most, leave the option for Background Render switched on and the Mac will take care of any rendering every time you stop work for a few seconds.

Use Original or Optimized Media

Leave this option set to Use Original or Optimized Media, unless you specifically want to work with low-resolution proxy media.

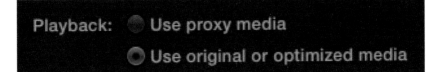

Playback: ● Use proxy media
           ◉ Use original or optimized media

Many formats, such as XDCAM EX, DVCPro HD, DV, and ProRes, can all be edited within Final Cut Pro X without requiring transcoding. However, for other codecs, such as AVCHD or H.264 (used widely in DSLRs), it is advisable to transcode, or optimize the footage, so that Final Cut Pro X can work with the content in a trouble-free way. By leaving the option checked to Use Original or Optimized Media means, if needed, the Final Cut Pro will optimize to ensure trouble-free performance. Otherwise, the media will be used in its native codec.

5

If footage needs to be transcoded, it is encoded as ProRes 4:2:2. ProRes is a high-quality mastering format, native to Final Cut Pro. It is a 10-bit 4:2:2 codec (often described as high bandwidth) and is scalable, with files working from offline Proxy to broadcast ProRes 4:2:2. For high-end production and motion graphics work, ProRes HQ is used; for super high-end and cinema production, ProRes 4:4:4 is the codec of choice.

The other option, Use Proxy Media, needs to be considered depending on the type of production you are doing.

Proxy media refers to low-resolution files designed to make the editing process quick and efficient, particularly for older or lower-spec Macs.

Playback: ⬤ **Use proxy media**

Using Proxy Media offers an offline way of working, at the press of a button. The cost, however, is that the Proxy Media needs to be generated, which takes time. So, think carefully as to whether you wish to work this way. If you have a project with 20 hours of footage, then creating 20 hours of Proxy Media is going to take quite a while.

The option to use Proxy Media is simply instructing Final Cut Pro X to use any Proxy Media which has been generated. If this media does not exist or is offline, then by selecting this option you will get warning indicators to show that the media is offline.

You are clearly warned when media is offline in Final Cut Pro X.

Playback Quality: Better Performance Versus High Quality

For playback of video, there are two choices: High Quality or Better Performance. High Quality will give you full-resolution images to view; however, performance in terms of playback will vary according to Mac used, processor speed, amount of RAM, and graphics card installed.

If you find performance isn't fluid, for example, the video and audio are stuttering or choppy on playback, or if you get a Dropped Frame warning, then switch to Better Performance. This will produce lower-quality video on playback, with less technical demands on the Mac. When you stop playback, you will see a high-resolution still.

You can easily switch between High Quality and Better Performance at any time.

Leave the option to Create Optimized Media for Multicam Clips checked. Multicam editing is very intensive in terms of system resources. So if you plan on editing Multicam, you need to let the computer optimize the media for playback.

Import Preferences

	Import
Editing Playback Import	

Organizing: ☐ Copy files to Final Cut Events folder
☑ Import folders as Keyword Collections

Transcoding: ☑ Create optimized media
☐ Create proxy media

Video: ☐ Analyze for stabilization and rolling shutter
☐ Analyze for balance color
☐ Find people
☐ Consolidate find people results
☐ Create Smart Collections after analysis

Audio: ☐ Analyze and fix audio problems
☐ Separate mono and group stereo audio
☐ Remove silent channels

Several of the Import Preferences are crucial to defining how you work with Final Cut Pro X. The first option is important: Copy Files to Final Cut Event Folder. If you leave this option checked, then every media file used in the project will be copied to the hard drive and stored in an area known as the Final Cut Events folder.

Effectively, you are leaving it to Final Cut Pro X to do all the media management for you.

The downside is you will consume a lot of hard drive space as the media will exist in its original location and also within the Final Cut Pro Events folder. While you could remove the original files, once copied, this is risky, in case something goes astray.

Rather than allow Final Cut Pro X to copy all the media, the method I chose is to leave the Copy Files to Final Cut Event Folder option unchecked. This applies when importing media which already exists on hard drive. If files are imported from memory card or tape, then you need to have Copy Media to Event Folder checked – this will then copy these files to the hard drive where the Events Folder is located.

Therefore, when importing existing files from hard drive (with Copy Files to Final Cut Events Folder unchecked), the original media is referenced by Final Cut Pro X. It is therefore important to be aware that if the original media is moved or deleted, then your project will no longer play. You can cause irreparable damage. Provided you are careful and go to the effort of putting the media in a folder, somewhere safe, then you should have no trouble.

The choice is to either let Final Cut Pro X copy the files to the Events folder or for you to define the location where the source files are located on the hard drive and then let Final Cut Pro X reference to these.

For myself, I want to define where my media files are stored and do not wish to double-up on media and add to time to the process by either transcoding or copying files. Therefore, I leave this option unchecked.

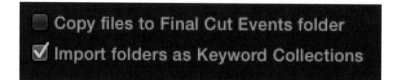

The second option for the import preferences is Import Folders as Keyword Collections.

I always leave this option checked. The importance of Keyword Collections will become clear when we begin editing and filing media. For this moment, be aware that naming the folder on hard drive before you import, it will result in the name of that folder being applied to the collection of the clips in what is known as a Keyword Collection.

Think of Keywording as providing the means to file and categorize clips by names or labels. More on this later!

Transcoding: I leave Create Optimized Media checked. This means any media which Final Cut Pro X decides is difficult to work with, such as AVCHD or H.264, will automatically be transcoded to ProRes on import. If the media can be easily worked with in its current form, then it will be left in its original state. Regardless, when transcoding files Final Cut Pro X always retains the original media for future use, so nothing is lost!

Create Proxy Media: Already described in the Playback Preferences is the ability to switch between full-resolution media and low-resolution ProRes Proxy files. For this to take place, the media must be transcoded. By leaving the option Create Proxy Media checked on import, the low-resolution or Proxy files will automatically be generated.

☑ Create proxy media

I tend to leave this option switched off. Working with smaller proxy files unde-niably will provide for better performance, but the expense is that these files need to be generated, which takes up time, system resources, and hard drive space.

■ Create proxy media

While in general I leave the Create Proxy Media option switched off, if you find your system is choking or stuttering whilst playing or outputting video, or if you have plenty of time and wish to experiment, then let Final Cut Pro X build the Proxies and you will get a feel for the result.

It is only the press of a button in the Playback Preferences to switch back and forth between

Playback: ● Use proxy media

Proxy and the original or optimized media. Be aware that because the Proxies run at a low data rate, rendering will be quicker and the speed of the system may well feel more responsive and fine tuned.

Simply put, it is easier for the computer to work with Proxy media than full-resolution files. The option to generate Proxy media and to switch between Proxy or full resolution is a simple way to achieve what used to take place first in an offline edit suite and then later in an expensive online edit suite.

Video: ☐ Analyze for stabilization and rolling shutter

☐ Analyze for balance color

☐ Find people

☐ Consolidate find people results

☐ Create Smart Collections after analysis

Audio: ☐ Analyze and fix audio problems

☐ Separate mono and group stereo audio

☐ Remove silent channels

What Apple gives you with Final Cut Pro X is a complete editing system. Do not underestimate the power of Final Cut Pro X. Compared to the suites of yesterday, this is a tremendously capable editing system with features we couldn't have even dreamed of.

The other options in Import Preferences I leave switched off. For my editing, I do not want the computer to analyze my footage for color balance, to look for audio problems, or to categorize shots for me. This takes up computing power as it processes the information. I'm interested in cutting. Let nothing slow me down.

Note: Leaving these options unchecked does not mean you lose the ability to perform these tasks. Each of the processes can all be done later during editing.

THE INTERFACE

MVI_5998   MVI_5999   MVI_6000   MVI_6001   MVI_6002

MVI_6013   MVI_6014   MVI_6015   MVI_6016   MVI_6017

MVI_6071   MVI_6087   MVI_6088   MVI_6089   MVI_6090

MVI_6101   MVI_6102   MVI_6103   MVI_6104   MVI_6105

MVI_6119   MVI_6120   MVI_6121   MVI_6122   MVI_6123

MVI_6134   MVI_6135   MVI_6136   MVI_6137   MVI_6138

The Three-Window Interface

The interface of Final Cut Pro X is split into three windows: the Event Library, the Viewer, and the Timeline.

The Event Library is where you access the media with which you build your edited movie. Here, all the clips, audio files, graphic elements, and music are filed away for you to access, in Filmstrip view or List view.

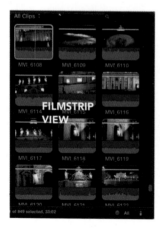

You can quickly toggle between Filmstrip view and List view by pressing the controls at the bottom of the Event Library.

Use the controls to switch between the two views

The Viewer: this is where you watch the camera original footage when playing clips in the Event Library; or where you view the edited movie by playing back in the Timeline.

Note: By clicking the bottom right of the window you can switch to full screen viewing. Press escape to get out of full screen view.

Timeline: you build your edited movie here. Shots, represented by blocks, are positioned and moved around in relation to other shots, thus enabling the editing process to take place. Clips can be viewed in different ways, audio can be separated from video, and tools can be used to perform different editing tasks.

You can switch between different views of the clips in the Timeline by using the Change Clip Appearance Controls (bottom right of the Timeline).

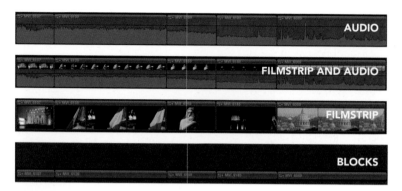

The appearance and size of the video and audio clips can be adjusted as needed. These views can be useful depending on the complexity of the edit and whether you are editing video, audio, or a combination of both.

The Five-Window Interface

The three-window interface can easily be extended to become a five-window interface. Two additional windows are now present: the Inspector and the Effects Browser.

The Inspector is a window you will refer to regularly. Here, parameters can be adjusted relating to the media you are working with in the Timeline or the Events Browser. You can adjust color correction and audio settings, crop, distort, and position the image, and switch on or off image stabilization.

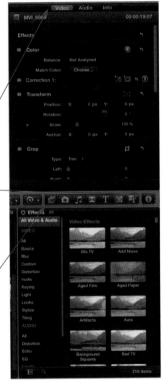

Three separate tabs can be accessed for video, audio, and media info.

The shortcut to call up the Inspector is Command + 4 or press the "i" symbol to the middle far right of the interface.

The Effects Browser provides a gateway to a wide range of sophisticated effects to draw upon. First-class chroma keying, luma keying, and a host of customizable and prebuilt options are offered. Everything from blurs to audio distortion can be accessed. Other tabs offer Titles, Transitions, and Generators.

Effects   Titles   Inspector
    Transitions Generators

Note: At any time you can return to the simplistic three-window interface by selecting the Window menu at the top of the interface. Scroll down and choose Revert to Original Layout. Most editing work will be done with either the three-window or five-window setup unless you are working with a dual monitor display.

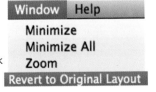

  You can also click on the Inspector icon or Effects icon to close these windows.

Working with Dual Monitor Displays

Twin monitor set-up with Events on second display

If you want to get serious when editing with Final Cut Pro X, invest in a second monitor. While not essential, it transforms the editing process from a confined, limited work area to an expansive area capable of dealing with large amounts of media.

For a large project, such as a documentary with 20 hours of footage or more, I wouldn't consider doing this with a single monitor setup. You need the space to review and organize the footage. Even for smaller projects, twin monitors, in my opinion, is the ideal way to work.

Select the Window menu at the top of the Interface and look at the options towards the bottom. There are two displays when working with dual monitors.

1. Show Events on Second Display: The Events Library is where you organize your footage. When dealing with hundreds or thousands of clips, a large work area is very desirable. A second monitor capable of 1920 x 1080 display is ideal.

   Show Events on Second Display
   Show Viewer on Second Display

2. Show Viewer on Second Display: Perfect for client viewing and also great for editing. The result is full-screen playback of raw or edited content, so you get a much better view than you will with the Viewer positioned small in the single-window interface.

   Show Events on Second Display

   Show Viewer on Second Display

The Final Cut Pro X interface on a single monitor can get quite crowded; therefore, the advantage of working with dual monitors is that there is room to spread out and be comfortable. The editing experience is not only more enjoyable, you get more done due to the enhanced work area.

Show Events on Second Display

The advantages should be clear. With this dual monitor setup, the Viewer and the Timeline are positioned on one monitor and the Event Library is displayed on the second monitor. Clips can be clearly viewed, labeled, and categorized, in either Filmstrip or List view. I find this display ideal and work with it a lot.

Main monitor shows viewer and timeline.

Second monitor shows event library.

Show Viewer on Second Display

For full-screen playback while viewing and editing, if you have fast enough drives and can work at high quality (set in Playback Preferences), then this is even better. This provides an effective way to achieve full-screen playback, with the Events Library and Timeline positioned on the main display. The large space for the Events Library provides for a good-size work area.

Main monitor shows events library and timeline.

Second monitor shows viewer full-screen.

IMPORTING MEDIA

  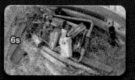 

9s GOPR7399   9s GOPR7400   10s GOPR7401   8s GOPR7402

GOPR7403   9s GOPR7404   8s GOPR7405   10s GOPR7406

GOPR7407   5s GOPR7408   10s GOPR7409   6s GOPR7410

7s   6s   5s

Hide Imported Clips   1 of 24 selected, 09:12   All

Stop Import   Close   Import Selected...

Ways to Import Media

There are two ways to bring media into Final Cut Pro X. The first is to import directly from a camera or the media card used inside the camera while filming. The other way is to import media from a hard drive which has already been converted to a format which Final Cut Pro X understands. A list of Final Cut Pro X supported cameras can be found at http://help.apple.com/finalcutpro/cameras/en/index.html?

If the camera you are working with is not in this list, don't panic! Many of the professional cameras are not supported directly by Final Cut Pro X. However, the means to convert the footage is often supplied via a capture or transfer utility provided by the camera manufacturer.

Importing Media from a Camera

Choose the File menu at the top of the interface, scroll down, and you will see the following two options:

 1   Import from Camera

 2   Import.

File   Edit   View   Mark

New Project...
Project Properties...

New Event
New Keyword Collection
New Folder

Import From Camera...   ⌘I
Import   ▶

 You can also press the Camera icon in the left middle of the interface to invoke the Import from Camera command.

Provided you have a camera which Final Cut Pro X recognizes, or the media mounted on your desktop, then the **Camera Import** window will open. Note: Camera Import works with many of the AVCHD cameras on the market; there is also a driver, available from Sony, which enables XDCAM EX files to be imported into Final Cut Pro X.

Each of the clips are represented in Filmstrip view. If you run the curser over the icons, you can skim through the clip. You may need to press the letter **S** to invoke the Skimming feature.

The simplest way to get the media onto the hard drive is to press the Import All command (at the bottom

Import All...

right of the Camera Import window). All of the clips will then be written to the hard drive where the Events folder is located. Note: you need to have Copy Media to Event Folder checked in Import Preferences.

You can also be selective about which clips are transferred. For a single clip, click to highlight

the clip of choice and press Import Selected.

Import Selected...

You can highlight a section of a single clip to import by either dragging the yellow ends to mark the range of media you wish to import or pressing the letter "i" for in and "o" for out to define the beginning and end points.

To import multiple clips, press the Command key (immediately left of the space bar) and click to highlight those clips you wish to import. Once the clips are highlighted, press Import Selected.

Import Selected...

Regardless of whether you choose to import a single clip, a section of a clip, multiple clips, or all of the clips, you need to define some crucial details before the media is written to drive.

○ Add to existing event:	FootageLibrary ⬍
⦿ Create new event:	ScotlandFootage
	Save to: FootageRick (169.0 GB free) ⬍

Transcoding:	☑ Create optimized media
	☐ Create proxy media
Video:	☐ Remove pulldown
	☐ Analyze for stabilization and rolling shutter
	☐ Analyze for balance color
	☐ Find people
	☐ Consolidate find people results
	☐ Create Smart Collections after analysis
Audio:	☐ Analyze and fix audio problems
	☐ Separate mono and group stereo audio
	☐ Remove silent channels

Cancel   Import

If you are starting a new project, I suggest you to create a New Event; if you are bringing material into integrate as part of an existing project, you may wish to add the media to an existing Event.

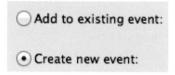

○ **Add to existing event:**

⦿ **Create new event:**

If you are creating a New Event, the crucial information you need to define is where you want the media to be stored. Click the arrows for the choice of available hard drives.

Macintosh HD (14.4 GB free)

FootageRick (169.0 GB free)

Save to ✓ Macintosh HD (14.4 GB free)

If you add to an existing Event, then the media will be stored on the same hard drive as the other media within the same Event.

As written in the Preferences chapter of this book, I strongly suggest leaving Create Optimized Media checked; this means if the footage is difficult to work with Final Cut Pro X will transcode this to a format which is "edit friendly," so to speak.

You don't need to create Proxy Media unless you specifically wish to work this way.

All the other options I leave unchecked.

Transcoding: ☑ Create optimized media
☐ Create proxy media

Video: ☐ Remove pulldown
☐ Analyze for stabilization and rolling shutter
☐ Analyze for balance color
☐ Find people
  ☐ Consolidate find people results
☐ Create Smart Collections after analysis

Audio: ☐ Analyze and fix audio problems
☐ Separate mono and group stereo audio
☐ Remove silent channels

Cancel | Import

Import | Press Import and the media will be written to the hard drive.

Importing Media from Hard Drive

Look to the Events Browser in Final Cut Pro X and observe that all connected hard drives are listed on the left of screen.

You can choose to store media on any connected drive.

In order to store media on a drive, it must be imported into an event. Think of an event as being an area where you store media to access; essentially it is similar to Bins in other editing programs. However, it is not the same. An Event is where you would file media that is related. You could, for example, choose for all the media of a project to be stored within an Event, or for all the camera footage for a day's shooting to be stored in an Event. Once footage is imported into an Event, it can be catalogued and categorized. This will be dealt with later.

Events are represented in purple and can be named however you wish.

To import media to hard drive, at least one event must exist. If there is no Event on a hard drive you wish to use, then you must create the Event.

To Create an Event

1 Click the hard drive of choice in the Event Library—this is important. The drive you choose defines where the media will be stored.

2 Scroll to File - New Event. The shortcut is Option + N. Alternatively, control-click on the hard drive of choice and select New Event.

File	Edit	View
New Project...		
Project Properties.		
New Event		

3   The Event will now be visible in purple and labeled "New Event" with the date.

▼ 🗂 March2012
⭐ New Event 6-04-2012

4   Click to highlight the Event; click again and overtype to give it a name.

▼ 🗂 March2012
▼ ⭐ Antarctica
🎬 Antarctica

Importing Media to an Event

There are three ways to import media to an event:

1   Highlight the Event and choose Import Files from the File menu.

Import   ▶   **Files...**

2   If the Event contains no media, select Import Files from within the Browser area.

New Event
New Folder
New Keyword Collection
New Smart Collection

Import Files...

Import Files

3   Control-click on the Event and choose Import Files.

When you Import you have the same choices to make, which we saw in the Camera Import window.

Once again, you need to decide your workflow.

You can create a New Event or add to an Existing Event.

Many of these choices were discussed in Preferences. For me, the crucial commands are to Import Folders as Keyword Collections, and, also, to Create Optimized Media.

Just to refresh what these options do:

- Importing Folders as Keyword Collections—this means that the name of the folder will be assigned to the collection of clips you are importing. The usefulness and relevance of Keywording will become clear in Chapter 4.

- Create Optimized Media—if the source media is difficult for Final Cut Pro X to work with, then the files will be transcoded to ProRes, which works native in Final Cut Pro X. AVCHD and H.264, for example, are difficult formats for the software to work with; thus, creating optimized media means the whole editing process will be easier for the computer to manage.

Add to existing Event: Antarctica

Create new Event:

Save to: FootageRick (169.0 GB free)

Organizing: ☐ Copy files to Final Cut Events folder
☑ Import folders as Keyword Collections

Transcoding: ☑ Create optimized media
☐ Create proxy media

Video: ☐ Analyze for stabilization and rolling shutter
☐ Analyze for balance color
☐ Find people
☐ Consolidate find people results
☐ Create Smart Collections after analysis

Audio: ☐ Analyze and fix audio problems
☐ Separate mono and group stereo audio
☐ Remove silent channels

As written already, the choice to Create Proxy Media depends on how powerful your computer is and the workflow you choose to employ.

The other choices I leave unchecked.

The Dashboard shows when the computer is working.

When you import media, you will get a display showing the files are being processed.

Look to the Dashboard and bang in the center of the interface—if you see a spinning wheel, you will know media is being processed. It may be that rendering is taking place, the computer may be generating thumbnails, or media may be transcoding. The Dashboard indicator will display a spinning circle or show a percentage symbol to show that work is being done in the background.

Click on the spinning wheel in the Dashboard to reveal which processes are taking place.

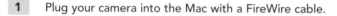

Capture from Tape

There is a third way to bring in media: Final Cut Pro X enables capture from DV, DVCAM, or HDV tape.

For those who shoot these formats, or those who have an archive to be accessed, this facility enables the media to be transferred to a hard drive. The transfer facility is basic but effective.

1 Plug your camera into the Mac with a FireWire cable.

2 Set the camera to VTR mode, then turn it on. Check that the camera is outputting the format you wish to capture, that is, DV/DVCAM or HDV. If the camera is not set correctly, the Final Cut Pro X will not see the video signal.

3 Turn your attention to Final Cut Pro X and press the camera icon or choose Import from Camera from the File menu.

4 The Camera Import window will open. Import From Camera.

Note: You can see that the FireWire device is recognized as it will appear in the list above Apple FaceTime. You can also capture direct from the built-in camera when using a laptop and record direct to hard drive.

5   Play the tape using the virtual VTR controller. Alternatively, use the Space Bar for start/stop, the letter J to spool backward (press J up to five times to spool), and the letter L to spool forwards (again incrementally up to five taps of the L key).

Press Import and you will see the familiar window prompting you to define several fields of information. Most important, define, if you wish, to Add Media to an Existing Event or to Create a New Event; if you Create a New Event, you need to define the hard drive where the media will be stored.

○ Add to existing event: New Event 7-04-2012

● Create new event: Antarctica

Save to: FootageRick   (168.9 GB free)

Transcoding: ☑ Create optimized media
            ☐ Create proxy media

Video: ☐ Remove pulldown
       ☐ Analyze for stabilization and rolling shutter
       ☐ Analyze for balance color
       ☐ Find people
          ☐ Consolidate find people results
       ☐ Create Smart Collections after analysis

Audio: ☐ Analyze and fix audio problems
       ☐ Separate mono and group stereo audio
       ☐ Remove silent channels

Cancel   Import

You can capture from DV/DVCAM or HDV tape in standard or widescreen aspect ratio.

If you wish to capture from tape formats beyond DV/DVCAM and HDV, then you need to look toward third-party providers for capture solutions. Companies such as AJA Video Systems, Blackmagic Design, and Matrox all offer capture utilities enabling capture from high-end professional decks.

ORGANIZATION

All Clips

336_1712_01

ame	Duration	Start	End
▶ 336_1953_01	00:01:51:32	05:29:58:34	05:
▶ 336_1951_01	00:00:56:32	05:27:49:40	05:
▶ 336_1950_01	00:00:12:28	05:27:37:12	05:
▶ 336_1949_01	00:00:11:56	05:27:25:16	05:
▶ 336_1948_01	00:00:26:50	05:26:58:26	05:
▶ 336_1715_01	00:00:49:00	03:59:45:20	04:
▶ 336_1714_01	00:00:26:00	03:59:19:20	03:
▶ 336_1713_01	00:00:12:32	03:59:07:04	03:
▶ 336_1712_01	00:00:22:50	03:58:44:14	03:

Getting Organized

Any film is literally built. Just as a novel will have chapters and subplots, each and every film has an underlying structure. The raw components needed to build the film are planned for in the scripting stage, gathered while filming, and structured during editing.

I liken the filmmaking process to making a set of chopsticks from a tree trunk. An entire tree can be whittled away to leave nothing remaining other than two small pieces of wood—these are the chopsticks. Film or video is the same. A mountain of footage is acquired and throughout the editing process this footage is chopped down to a fraction of its original size to leave a small, yet refined, remnant of the original content.

In simple terms, editing is nothing more than putting shots and sounds together. In reality, it is much more than this. It is both a technical and a creative process. It is also intuitive. Anyone can string words together, but not everyone is able to write a good story or a good book without a sound knowledge of language. Editing is similar.

To make the editing process efficient and streamlined, you need to be organized. Organization is the key to building, refining, and sculpting a film. You need to know where those clips are, how to access them, and how to get them into the Timeline to hit the mark every time. There are many tools within Final Cut Pro X to help you to organize your footage. The process of getting organized begins with reviewing your footage.

Reviewing Footage

1   Select an Event in the Event Library and click any of the clips in the Event. The clip you select will then show in the Viewer.

2   Press the Space Bar and the clip will play. Press the Space Bar again to stop.

3   You can also use the letters J, K, and L to review footage. By tapping J or L, the footage will play, then speed up, incrementally, each time you press the key (up to five taps).

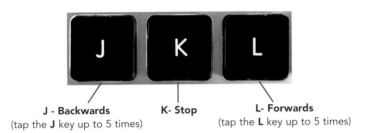

J - Backwards
(tap the **J** key up to 5 times)

K- Stop

L- Forwards
(tap the **L** key up to 5 times)

4 Perhaps the easiest way to look through a clip is to use the Skimming function. Simply point the curser towards any of the clips in the Event Library and drag across it. You will see the clip

zip past in fast motion in the Viewer as you drag. If this doesn't work, press the letter S to activate Skimming.

Drag across clips in the Event Library and see the result in the Viewer

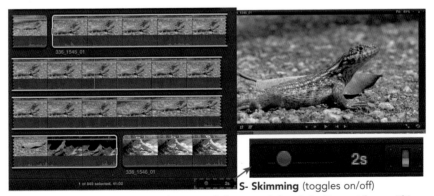

S- Skimming (toggles on/off)

Expand the filmstrip size using the controls bottom right of the Event Library. This gives you fine control while skimming over a clip.

- S: Skimming (toggles on/off)

- Shift + S: Skimming without audio (toggle on/off)

Use the above shortcuts or use the Skimming controls in the middle/right of the interface.

Skimming on/off   **Audio Skimming on/off**

Note: When using the Skimming feature you can drag across several clips; you don't need to do this one at a time.

With several clips lined up in the Event Library, skim across as many as you wish to see the footage displayed in the Viewer.

Rating Footage

The ability to rate your footage provides a fantastic means to weed out the good footage from the bad. Clips can be marked as Favorites, Rejects, or left unrated.

You don't have to rate your footage. If you have a photographic memory and can remember everything by the sheer power of thought, then fantastic for you; however, most of us need to constantly review the media to remind us where everything is. Being able to mark specific clips as good or bad can be very useful.

Below the Event Library, notice two stars and a red cross. These are your rating tools.

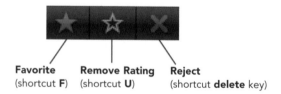

Favorite (shortcut **F**)   **Remove Rating** (shortcut **U**)   **Reject** (shortcut **delete** key)

Highlight a clip in the Event Viewer and skim through it. Decide whether the clip is one you want to use or is one you want to reject.

If it is a clip you wish to mark as a Favorite, press the green star below the Event Library or press the letter F. If you are in Filmstrip view, a green line will appear within the clip. If you are in List view - click the triangle to the left of the clip you marked and Favorite will be marked below the clip.

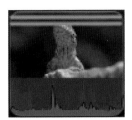

Green line indicates Favorite

Should you wish to mark a clip as a Reject press the red X or the Delete key. In Filmstrip view, the clip is marked red; in List view, this is indicated below the clip as a red X.

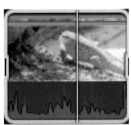

Red line indicates Reject

There is a good reason to go to the effort of marking clips as Favorites or Rejects.

Note: The blue line you can see marked in each of the clips represents that a Keyword has been added to that clip. Keywording is dealt with later in this chapter.

Click the drop-down menu in the top left corner of the Event Viewer interface and you see options to sort media within the event.

You can choose to Hide Rejected clips, immediately eliminating anything from view which you have marked as Rejected.

You can also choose to show only Favorites - those clips you have marked as being good takes.

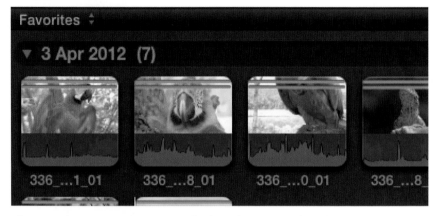

Alternatively, you can choose to only show the Rejected media - perhaps you are deep into editing and need just one more shot... so you start looking through the media which you initially rejected.

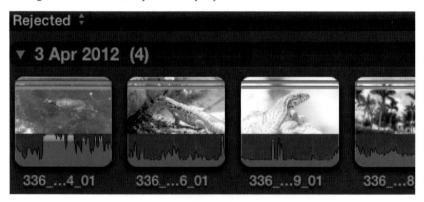

I'm sure the advantages are clear of being able to rate and show only the Favorites or hide the Rejected clips. Effectively what Apple has created is a functional database geared to define footage as good or bad.

You can choose to use or reject this functionality. I find it useful and it gets much deeper than simply marking clips as Favorites or Rejects.

Remember to reset to All Clips, as the setting you choose will remain until you change it, even when you move between different Events.

Marking Sections within Clips

Not only you mark Favorites and Rejects, you can also selectively mark sections within clips as Favorites or Rejects, and then use the sort options to show only the portions of the clip you specify.

This is particularly useful when dealing with long clips. For example, a 20-minute interview can be marked up at the most relevant places, or a three-hour conference record could be marked for the highlights of the piece only.

Here's how it works:

1 Skim through a clip in the Events Browser.

2 Click on the clip then drag the yellow range markers to define the area you wish to select. Alternatively, use the letter "i" for in and "o" for out to define the area.

Drag the yellow range markers to define the range within the clip or press the letters I O F in succession to mark a range selection.

3 Press F to mark this section as a Favorite or press the letter R to mark as Rejected. Alternatively, use the green star for favorite and red cross for reject.

As you mark the sections, observe that only the portions you defined are marked as a Favorite or Reject.

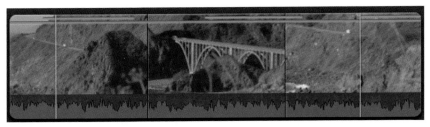

Multiple favorites marked within a single clip.

A mixture of Favorites and Rejects can be marked within a single clip.

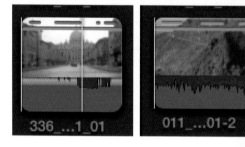

Name	Duration	Start	En
▼ 336_3927_01	00:04:08:20	08:23:25:22	08
FootageLibraryRick	00:04:08:20	08:23:25:22	08
X Rejected	00:00:18:29	08:23:33:45	08
★ Favorite	00:00:41:16	08:24:02:34	08
X Rejected	00:00:16:32	08:24:59:44	08
★ Favorite	00:01:01:20	08:25:33:32	08
X Rejected	00:00:32:23	08:26:45:12	08

Note the different views: List view (above) and filmstrip (left). Favorites and rejects are clearly marked.

You can then selectively display Favorites or Rejects from the filtering choices at the top right of the Event Viewer.

All Clips
Hide Rejected
No Ratings or Keywords
✓ **Favorites**
Rejected

It should be clear that the ability to mark clips and sections within clips as Favorites or Rejects, and then be able to sort this information, is of tremendous benefit, particularly when you are dealing with a lot of media, or when many long takes have been recorded. You can mark entire takes as good or bad or sections within takes.

This ability to mark and sort is one of the great strengths of Final Cut Pro.

Labeling and Searching Clips

In all the images shown so far, each of the clips have had names assigned by the camera during filming.

None of these numbers mean very much, other than being a sequential naming of the clips.

Final Cut Pro X offers powerful means to name and then search through all of the named clips. You can also easily add comments which can be searched, and, if you wish, you can Batch Rename clips. In terms of being organized, this is of huge importance. You can quickly search through all of the Events on your computer to locate any of the named clips.

Labeling clips is easy. You can work in either Filmstrip or List view.

1	Click on a clip to highlight, then click on the naming area so you can overtype.
2	Type a name relevant to the clip.
3	Press return.
4	Repeat the process for other clips in the Event which you wish to rename.

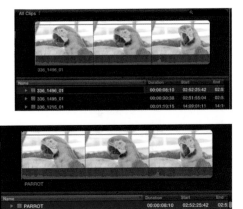

In the following images, there are several different views of a lizard. Each has been individually named by following the above steps. The real magic is in the search abilities of Final Cut Pro X. Each of the clips that has been named is searchable; therefore, if we key in the word "lizard" into the search criteria in the top left of the Event Browser, then any matching items will be found.

41

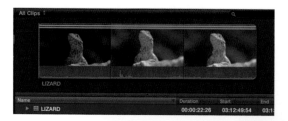

Each of the clips has been named so that it can be searched through using the database capabilities of Final Cut Pro X.

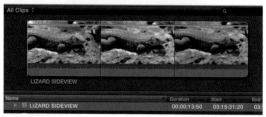

Key in the search criteria (top left of the Events Browser) and matching items will be displayed in either List or Filmstrip view.

Above: the search criteria displayed in Filmstrip view.

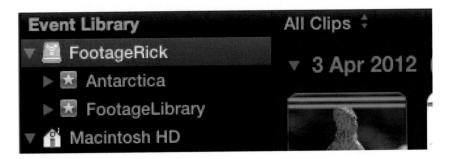

It is important to be aware that every time you search, the results will be displayed according to whether you click a hard drive or an Event.

In the above image, the hard drive Rick has been selected, therefore any search which you invoke applies to everything on this hard drive. If an Event is highlighted, then only the Event will be a searched.

Always remember to clear the information in the Search Field once you have completed a search—otherwise, the search criteria remains in place.

Adding Notes to Clips

Notes can be just as useful as adding name labels to your clips. Quite often, when scanning through footage, I will stop and add a quick comment to a clip. It may be as simple as "great shot" or "definitely use," or something more specific like "nice light - evening," or perhaps "use in end sequence."

Anything that will stick in my memory which I can then key into the search field to retrieve the shot when I need it.

Go into List view in the Events Browser; observe that there are several columns extending to the right. You can scroll to reveal more columns.

Find the column titled Notes.

Content Created	Roles	Notes
6 Jun 2011 05:46:49	Video, Dialogue ▼	
6 Jun 2011 05:46:41	Video, Dialogue ▼	

Scroll right in the Events Browser to find the column Notes.

Name ▲	Notes	Duration
▼ 3 Apr 2012 (4)		
▶ ▦ Rome 1		00:00:13:23
▶ ▦ Rome 2		00:00:08:01
▶ ▦ Rome 3		00:00:19:01
▶ ▦ Rome 4		00:00:23:10

Click and drag so the Notes column sits next to the Name column.

Rome 1

me ▲	Notes	Duration	Start
3 Apr 2012 (4)			
▶ ▦ Rome 1	St Peter's Basilica	00:00:13:23	08:27:30:00
▶ ▦ Rome 2		00:00:08:01	08:27:11:00
▶ ▦ Rome 3		00:00:19:01	08:27:55:00
▶ ▦ Rome 4		00:00:23:10	08:26:26:00

Click in the Notes column (to the right of any of the clips) and type information. You can enter anything from a word to detailed descriptions.

Everything you type becomes searchable information. Once you have entered information for several clips, then type a word you wish to search for into the Search Criteria area, at the top right of the Events Browser.

All of the information entered as notes is searchable.

The clips with matching results will then be displayed for you to work with.

Note how the order of search takes place. If you click on an Event, then that Event will be searched. If you click on a hard drive, then the entire drive will be searched.

You have powerful database capabilities at your fingertips to search through notes and clip names, provided you go to the effort of organizing and marking up your footage.

Batch Renaming of Clips

The ability to Batch Rename clips in Final Cut Pro X is a fantastic means for the editor to organize their footage, not just because naming conventions like 013_0251_01 for camera originals is meaningless and useless, but also because clips which you have renamed are searchable.

Think of the potential of being able to search a database, with clips named by you, in a project with hundreds of clips or more. Batch renaming involves selecting 5, 10, 100, or as many clips as you wish within an Event. You need to set the naming convention and then instruct Final Cut Pro to rename the clips you have chosen. Once done, you can search through all Events stored on the drive to access the named clips in one place.

1 To Batch Rename clips, you need to first set the naming convention. Open the Inspector by pressing the "i" symbol or Command + 4.

2 In the Info tab of the Inspector, click the Gear icon in the lower right. Scroll to Apply Custom Name and then choose Edit.

3 You will be greeted with a very complicated window, shown below. Click to choose the second option on the left, which is Custom Name with Counter.

4 Click in the Custom Name box and type the naming convention you wish to use. Notice the increments you define will start at the number 1 unless you choose otherwise.

5 Now highlight a number of clips in any of your Events.

6 Again choose the gear icon in the Inspector and scroll to Apply Custom Name and then choose Custom Name with Counter.

The clips which you highlighted have then been renamed in the Event.

7 Repeat the process to change the naming preset and then you can Batch Rename other groups of clips. You can now search through all of the clips on any of drives connected to your Mac.

8 Click to highlight a drive. Type the search criteria into the top right of the Events Library. Final Cut will then search through all  the events on the drive you have selected and you can then view the clips that match the name you have applied.

▶ 🖼 Chicken 1	03:14:18:28	03:14:41:32	00:00:23:04	13 Aug 2011 12:07:57
▶ 🖼 Chicken 2	03:14:41:32	03:15:07:32	00:00:26:00	13 Aug 2011 12:08:31
▶ 🖼 Chicken 3	03:15:07:32	03:15:25:22	00:00:17:40	13 Aug 2011 12:08:53
▶ 🖼 Chicken 4	03:15:25:22	03:16:22:02	00:00:56:30	13 Aug 2011 12:11:34
▶ 🖼 Chicken 5	03:16:22:02	03:16:41:48	00:00:19:46	13 Aug 2011 12:13:19
▶ 🖼 Chicken 6	03:16:41:48	03:17:18:28	00:00:36:30	13 Aug 2011 12:14:25
▶ 🖼 Chicken 7	03:17:18:28	03:17:35:06	00:00:16:28	13 Aug 2011 12:14:55
▶ 🖼 Chicken 8	03:17:35:06	03:17:44:30	00:00:09:24	13 Aug 2011 12:15:27
▶ 🖼 Chicken 9	03:17:44:30	03:19:45:32	00:02:01:02	13 Aug 2011 12:17:47
▶ 🖼 Chicken 10	03:19:45:32	03:22:55:24	00:03:09:42	13 Aug 2011 12:21:13
🎞 ChickenCompile	00:00:00:00	00:06:29:04	00:06:29:04	13 Aug 2011 13:18:11

Clips that match the search criteria can then be viewed as either Filmstrip or Text. You therefore have a very simple means to Batch Rename clips and search through all of your Events to find exactly what you want, according to the naming structure you have chosen.

Keywording

If you want to get really sophisticated with the organization of your media, step into the world of Keywording. I think of rating footage, or marking Favorites and Rejects, as being a simple way to organize your footage. Keywording gives you far greater power.

Do not feel under pressure to keyword. Many editors are happy to break footage up into labeled events, perhaps rate or define sections as Favorites, and leave it as it. The power of Keywording is that within a single Event you can break your footage into defined sections, known as Keyword Collections. Think of Keyword Collections as a means to file footage away, or to break it into manageable, accessible groups.

Keywording can be applied to an entire clip, a range within a clip, or a group of clips.

Adding Keywords is done through what is known as the Keyword Editor.

1 Highlight a clip or group of clips to which you wish to apply the Keyword.

2 Open the Keyword Editor by clicking the icon that resembles a key in the Toolbar or press Command + K. Click the arrow to reveal the full list of Keywords that have been entered.

3 Highlight a clip or group of clips in the Event Browser, enter the Keyword into the Keyword Editor, and press return. You will then see animation as Keywords are applied to those clips you have highlighted.

There may be a pause while this takes place. If you have highlighted 50 clips or more, the pause may be several seconds.

4 Once the keywords have been added, notice that in Filmstrip View, a blue line has been added to the clip, indicating that the Keyword has been applied.

In List view, there is a triangle to the left of each clip. Click this to reveal Keywords associated with the media.

Keyword Collections in blue

Keyword collections appear within an Event in blue to the left of the Event Browser. Click on any of the collections to reveal the clips within the collection. Effectively, Keywording provides the means to file away and access media.

Keywords can also be added using shortcuts. First, open the  Keyword Editor, then press the triangle to reveal the list of Keywords; the shortcut is located to the left of each of the Keywords.

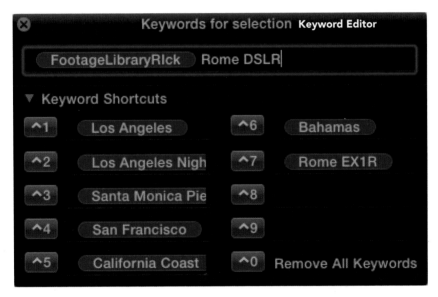

To apply any Keywords already entered to a clip or group of clips, simply press the shortcut, or use the keyboard to type Control + the number.

When many Keyword collections have been added, you end up with many categories, defined by yourself, where media is filed away. Be aware, Keyword Collections apply to a single Event, therefore, it can make sense to put all related media, or even all the media for a project into a single Event, and then break it up into Keyword Collections.

In many ways, Keywording can be used in the same way that Bins were used in the previous versions of Final Cut Pro (versions 1 to 7).

Keywording can be applied to groups of clips, individual clips, or a range within a clip. To apply to a range in a clip, the procedure is the same as already described, the difference being you use the yellow range selectors to define the area in the clip before applying the Keyword.

Drag the yellow ends to mark a range or key in "i" for in and "o" for out.

As stated earlier, you do not have to Keyword your media. However, once you get the concept of Keywording you will find, particularly on a project with lots of media, that this can be a great timesaver. Once upon a time, the only way to log your footage was to write notes, watch footage in real time, and jot down timecode numbers. Keywording provides a sophisticated means to log your footage, file it away, and retrieve it when you need to get to it quickly.

In summary, notice an entire chapter, close to 20 pages, has been devoted to organization. That is, because it is essential for the editor to be organized. You can't edit a production effectively without being organized.

Many years ago, in tape suites, the method was a paper edit with burnt-in timecode as a reference. The producer would come into the edit suite with pages of notes after having worked through the raw material in an offline suite or even viewing on VHS tape. Edit suites were expensive, so the time needed in these rooms was minimized.

Now, we have a world of tools to prepare, organize, and edit our media. The temptation may be to skip the organizing and sorting of footage, avoid key-words, and add notes or clip names. My view is that it is counterproductive for you not to be organized. I use a combination of all the methods described: Keywording, Batch Renaming, and adding notes to clips. This proves to be incredibly useful throughout the editing process. I regard the organization phase as laying the foundation for the edit. Spend the time getting organized and the rest of the edit will fall together.

00:01:18:00   00:01:20:00   00:01:22:00

EDITING

Editing is, without doubt, one of the most wonderfully creative art forms of the twentieth century, and has evolved into a universal means of expression in the twenty-first century. Previously, editing was restricted to those who worked in TV stations, those who worked in the film industry, and independent filmmakers, groups, and companies. Now, it's a totally different scene. Twenty-first century editing gives the tools to anyone to create amazingly high-quality video.

Jump back 30 or 40 years. If you or anyone wanted to create moving images, you were most likely going to be working on Super 8. Super 8 was affordable, accessible, and referred to as spaghetti by the professionals. The quality was one-quarter that of 16 mm, which, itself, was one-quarter the quality of 35 mm. So working with Super 8 was not only fiddly and awkward, but in terms of the tiny size of each frame, the quality suffered.

Working with Final Cut Pro X the quality does not suffer! This is a capable editing system which outputs many high-end codecs, including ProRes at either standard, HQ, LT, or even ProRes 4:4:4. ProRes is a high-quality mastering format with several levels of quality:

ProRes LT:	100 mbps
ProRes standard:	145 mbps
ProRes HQ:	220 mbps
ProRes 4:4:4:	Cinema quality

ProRes 4:4:4 is cinema quality—get that? This is a big deal. Back in the days of editing Super 8 or 16 mm anyone would have jumped at this opportunity.

I've made this point simply to demonstrate the power of the system you have in front of you. Whether you are a new user or a professional with years of experience, Final Cut Pro X enables you to produce content at the highest levels.

Regardless of the level at which you work, the mechanics behind postproducing your movie are the same.

The Process

Before we begin editing, let us quickly run through the process. Whether you're editing a home movie or a feature film, the process is the same.

i	Get footage onto hard drive.
ii	Review and look at the footage, get to know it, file it, and categorize it so you can extract what you need.
iii	Do a picture edit, meaning cut it all together. Often, a soundtrack and picture edit are built at the same time.
iv	Attend to audio—do what you can to make it sound good.
v	Add effects. This may also be done during the editing process. Effects can be as simple as a basic title to complex, multilayered effects which have been carefully built and constructed. Final Cut Pro X offers a wide range of fully built and customizable effects.
vi	Output—you may need to output a high-resolution QuickTime file, an H.264 encode, DVD, or Blu-ray. The means to output at a professional level is fully provided.

So far, we have covered getting footage on to the hard drive, reviewing, and organizing the footage.

Now, the time has come to start the editing process.

Creating a New Project

This is a very simple and essential procedure. You need to create a project—your movie, your edit, your Timeline—whatever you want to call it, the project contains all the information which makes up the edited content.

 1   Press the film icon lower left of the Timeline to show the project library.

The Project Library window slides into view, showing all the hard drives connected to your system. Projects are listed below each of the hard

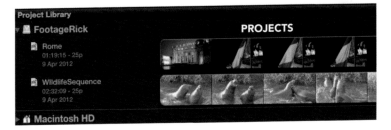

drives (if you have any projects already created) and these are also displayed in the Filmstrip view.

2   Control-click a hard drive where you wish to store the new project and choose File → New Project. Alternatively, press Command + N, or click the + symbol at the base of the Timeline.

Project Library

Footag...

New Project ⌘N
Rome   New Folder ⇧⌘N

File Edit View Mark Clip M

New Project... ⌘N

What you are doing is defining where the project will be stored on the hard drive. Note: This can be separated from the Event Library where you organize your media. My advice is to keep the projects and events on the same drive!

3   You will be greeted with a window which gives you choices to define the name and video properties of the project. Pay particular attention to the video properties. You can choose to set automatically based on the first video clip, or you can choose custom.

The easy way is to let Final Cut Pro decide and leave the video properties to set automatically based on the first video clip. This means the choice will be made for you. However, easy is not always best!

Final Cut Pro

Name: Rome2012

Default Event: FootageLibrary

Starting Timecode: 00:00:00:00

Video Properties: ● Set based on first video clip

○ Custom

Audio and Render Properties: ● Use default settings
Surround, 48kHz, ProRes 422
○ Custom

Use Automatic Settings   Cancel   OK

You need to know what format and frame rate you wish to output. In the world of HD, there are two main standards: 1280 x 720 or 1920 x 1080 (often called 720P and 1080P), and each of these can run at different frame rates.

By letting Final Cut Pro X automatically set the video properties based on first clip, this means if you edit a 1920 x 1080 as the first clip into the Timeline, then the result will be you will be editing a 1920 x 1080 project (at the frame rate of the first clip dropped into the Timeline).

If the first clip is 1280 x 720, then you will effectively be setting the project to be a 1280 x 720 project. It may be that you are working with 4:3 DV footage—again, if the first clip is set to this standard, then that is the image size which will be set.

Video Properties: ⦿ **Set based on first video clip**

Very often projects are made up of a mixture of footage—some HD, some SD, and perhaps a mixture of widescreen and standard aspect ratio. Furthermore, some footage may be shot at 25 frames per second, other footage at 29.97, and perhaps some at 24P. If you let the computer set the video properties automatically, then you need to make sure the first clip you edit into the Timeline is of the frame size and frame rate you wish to output to.

The idea of letting the computer set the video properties automatically is designed to make life easy, not complex. If all or the majority of the footage you are working with is of one standard, then allowing this to be set automatically can be a good idea.

There are times when it is advantageous to set the video properties manually. This gives you power to define the format, frame size, and frame rate.

Manually Setting Up a Project

I often choose to work this way. By manually setting up the project you can define details such as format, resolution, and frame rate.

Name: Rome2012

Default Event: FootageLibrary

Starting Timecode: 00:00:00:00

Video Properties: ○ Set based on first video clip
⦿ Custom
1080p HD | 1920x1080 | 25p
Format | Resolution | Rate

⦿ Custom
1080p HD | 1920x1080 | 25p
Format | Resolution | Rate

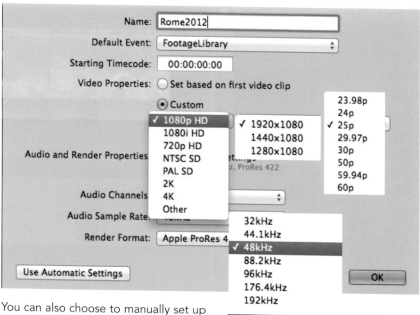

You can also choose to manually set up the audio and you can define the render format.

If these settings, numbers, frame rates, and different standards are completely confusing to you, then you need to stick to automatic. For those who have a good technical understanding of video production, setting up a project manually can often be the best way forward.

Once the project settings have been chosen, make sure the project is named, and press OK. You are now ready to move onto your first edit.

Basic Cutting

As already described, there are three areas you need to work among: the Events Library, the Viewer, and the Timeline.

You access clips in the Events Library, you watch these in the Viewer, and then you edit into the Timeline; and it is there the building blocks which represent the clips of your edit are organized.

1 Choose a clip inside one of the events.

2   Click on the clip and skim through it (press S if Skimming does not work).

3   Define a range within the clip by dragging either of the yellow ends or by pressing I and O.

EMPTY TIMELINE

4   Once a range is defined, look to the empty Timeline. Press the letter E. You will see the shot you highlighted in the Events Browser has been edited into the Timeline. How this is represented in the Timeline is determined by the view you have set for the Clip Appearance.

A SINGLE SHOT HAS BEEN EDITED INTO THE TIMELINE

5 Repeat the procedure—select a shot, view by skimming, mark a range, press the letter E (for Edit or for End) and the next shot will be edited to the end of the Timeline. The type of edit is referred to as an Append edit.

2 SHOTS EDIT INTO THE TIMELINE

6 Repeat the procedure until you will have several shots cut together in the Timeline.

SEVERAL SHOTS IN THE TIMELINE

Note: If you highlight several clips in the Event Browser and press E, then these are edited in order to direct the Timeline.

Notice that each clip is made up of video and audio. Video and audio are locked together, indicating the synchronization of image and sound.

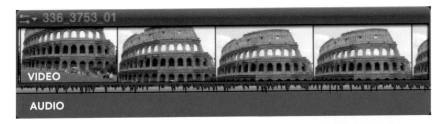

Clips can be displayed in several different way according to the option you have chosen for the clip appearance.

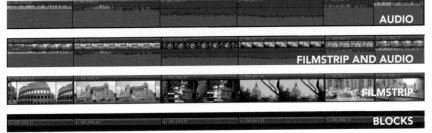

Sliding Clips around in the Timeline

You will now have several clips in the Timeline. These are in the order which you edited them. This ordering can quickly and easily be rearranged.

You can use the slider bottom right on the Timeline window to adjust the spread of the clips in the Timeline. This only affects the appearance, not duration.

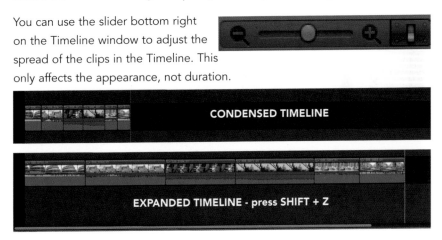

Press Shift + Z to fit the entire contents of the Timeline into the available space. Doing this makes it easy to get an overview of everything that has been edited into the Timeline.

To rearrange the shots simply click on a clip, drag it to a new position within the Timeline between two other clips, and release your mouse button. The clip will slide into place and the edits around it will slide left or right to accommodate. This is what Apple calls the magnetic Timeline.

Drag a clip to a new position within the Timeline.

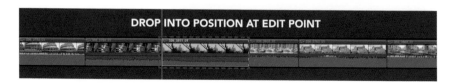

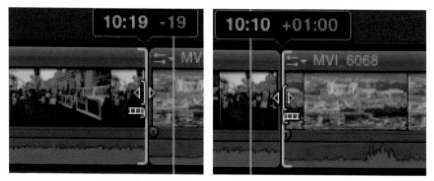

As well as dragging to rearrange, you can also adjust the duration of a clip by clicking to select and then dragging the yellow indicator on the end of the clip in either direction.

Extend/reduce clips by dragging left or right.

You can make the clip shorter from either end, essentially trimming away media, or, if media is available, you can extend the edit from either the beginning or the end, and therefore make it longer. An indicator will display in seconds and frames the change in duration.

It is important to understand the concept of available media. The representation in the Timeline of a clip refers to a media file which exists on the hard drive. Much of the time while editing you will use a portion of a shot but not the whole shot—there is still media available on the hard drive which can be accessed. If the full duration of the clip has been used, then there is no further media to draw on. You will know when you reach the limit of available media as you will not be able to extend the clip further. The yellow bracket will turn red to indicate that you have run out of media.

Separating Audio from Video

Each clip is made up of video and audio that is locked together. This will be obvious if you have set the clip appearance to Filmstrip view with waveforms visible. To edit to a high level, you need to be able to separate video from audio at will. Any professional editor knows this. Your film needs to be built from the ground up with attention to the soundtrack as well as the picture edit. Picture and sound do not always need to stick together.

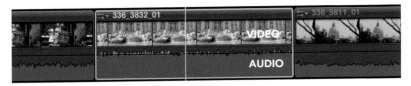

Separating audio from video is a fundamental need and enables you to then create a separate sound and picture edit. Sometimes picture and sound need to be locked; sometimes they need to be separated.

1 Click to highlight the clip with which you wish to work.

2 Go to the Clip menu—at the top of the interface, click and scroll to Detach Audio (shortcut: Control/Shift + S).

3   The result will be obvi-
    ous. Audio, represented
    in green, now appears
    separate from video.
    The Filmstrip view
    represents the video.

One can see clearly that the
audio is separated from the
video. If you click to select
the audio, you can move this
independent to the video.

Look to the point where the video and audio are joined. This shows
the audio is connected to the video. Whenever you move the video
clip, the connected audio will move with it. If you select Audio Only,
then you can move this independent of video.

Audio was always worked with separately in professional cutting rooms, from the
film days right to tape and nonlinear. In videotape suites, we used to bounce tracks
and do mix-downs; this gave us the means of working with audio separate from
video. In building a soundtrack, the editor needs to be able to take the audio and
use it in an entirely different way to how it was originally filmed with the image.

So, for simple editing leaving video and audio locked together may work just
fine—for more involved editing one needs greater flexibility.

Note: There is another function accessed from
the Clip menu: Expand Audio/Video. This
performs a very different function than detaching
audio.

Expand Audio/Video gives a visual representation of the video and audio. This can be quickly achieved by double-clicking any audio in the Timeline.

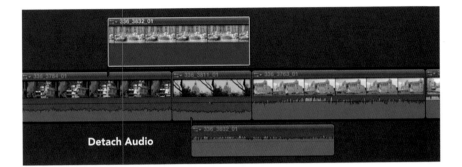

Detach Audio truly separates the audio and video so they can be worked with independently.

The Concept of Connected Clips

Final Cut Pro X does several different types of editing. The first method we discussed is invoked by pressing the letter E. This is called an Append edit—this edits shots onto the end of the Timeline. Therefore, what you are adding to the Timeline does not interfere with existing content in the Timeline.

The next type of edit creates what is called a Connected Clip. The Connect edit places a clip above another clip; it can be seen as a super impose edit. To perform a Connect edit, press the letter Q.

1 Mark a range within a clip within an event. Alternatively, click to select the entire clip.

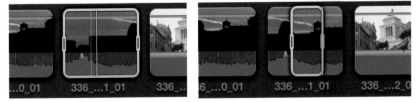

Either mark the entire clip or a range within the clip.

2 In the Timeline, click to position where you want the edit to take place. I suggest you keep Skimming on. If need be, press S or the icon which toggles Skimming on/off.

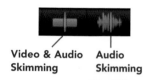

Video & Audio   Audio
Skimming   Skimming

Scrubber Bar

Skimmer

Note: With Skimming switched on the edit will take place wherever the Skimmer is positioned. With Skimming switched off edits take place wherever the Playhead is positioned.

3 With the Skimmer positioned where you want the edit to take place, press the letter Q.

The clip selected in the Event Library is the edited into the Timeline. The result is the clip is positioned one level up from the video which already exists. Notice the clip is attached to the clip beneath it—it is connected.

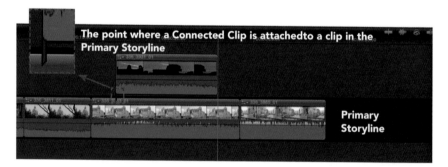

The point where a Connected Clip is attached to a clip in the Primary Storyline

Primary Storyline

Connected Clips are always edited either above or below what is called the Primary Storyline. The Primary Storyline is indicated in a dark shade of gray in the Timeline.

I think of the Primary Storyline as being the main story—this is the hardcore structure of your edit. What you add above as video, and below as audio, is secondary to the main story. It is as if the Primary Storyline is the foundation of your movie, with rest being built from there.

4   Edit several Connected Clips into the Timeline.

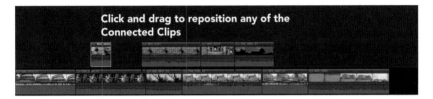

5   Click to select a Connected Clip and it can be moved and positioned. If you collide with another Connected Clip, then the clip you are moving will shift up a level, on top of the one it collides with.

Position Connected Clips where ever you wish by dragging.

Connected Clips can be positioned above or below the Primary Storyline. Most often you will see video as Connected Clips above the Primary Storyline, and audio below; however, there is no reason why you can't position video and/ or audio above or below the Primary Storyline. They can be dragged to either location.

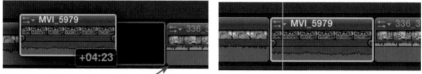

To move a Connected Clip into the Primary Storyline drag it to the point where two clips meet; then the clip you are positioning will slide into place.

Drag the Connected Clip between two clips in the Primary Storyline.

The clip will then slide into place.

To drag a clip from the Primary Storyline and make it into a Connected Clip simply drag it up or down. This then becomes a Connected Clip and the gap in the Primary Storyline closes; this is the Magnetic Timeline in action.

Furthermore, when dragging Connected Clips vertically you can prevent the clip from moving horizontally by holding down the Shift key while you drag.

**Hold Shift + Drag to move the Connected Clip vertically;
this maintains horizontal positioning.**

Directing the Flow of Video and Audio

So far we have done two types of edits:

1   The letter E, which is the Append edit; this edits clips directly onto the end of the Timeline.

2   The letter Q, which does a Connected Clip edit above or below the Primary Storyline.

It can be a real problem to do an edit and then have audio competing from two separate tracks. You need to be able to silence audio at will.

There are two ways: first, edit the picture only so the audio doesn't actually get edited into the Timeline; second, once audio has been edited, set the level to zero so that the audio cannot be heard.

Let's start with editing picture only without audio.

In the Toolbar in the middle of the interface, there are three icons which relate to the editing process.

These are for:

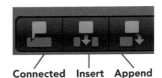

Connected   Insert   Append

1   Connected Clip, which we already discussed

2   Insert, still to be discussed

3   Append, which we already covered

The drop-down arrow reveals choices to switch video and/or audio on or off.

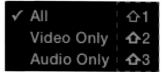

Quickly and easily you can choose to edit All (both video and audio) or Video Only or Audio Only.

The ability to channel video and audio separately or together is what is needed to fulfill the needs of the creative process. Since image and sound were first cut together editors the world over have been doing the same thing over and over, be it on film, tape, spinning disc, solid state, or whatever the medium may be. The means to achieving results changes with each turn of technology, yet the needs and the essential techniques are the same.

Editing Video Only or Audio Only is the means to achieving the results needed for professional-level work. You can edit the

picture over an interview and hear the existing soundtrack; you can introduce traffic sound, for example, to cover up an audio join; you can add sound effects, music, narration, or a video cutaway without affecting the soundtrack. This is how editors work.

Notice the shortcuts—embed this in your brain to speed up the process:

- Option + 1: Video and Audio
- Option + 2: Video Only
- Option + 3: Audio Only

You can fly through the editing process directing the edit so only video, audio, or both are edited at will.

Insert Editing

When editing you always have a choice - to push media forward and therefore extend the overall duration of the Timeline, or to add media to the Timeline without affecting the duration (meaning the duration stays the same), that is, the content is edited over existing media.

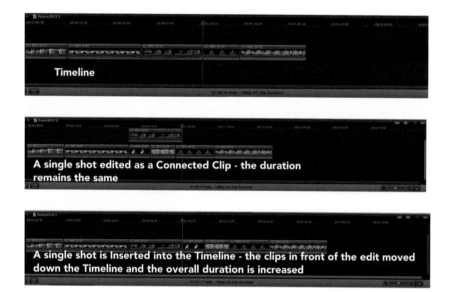

Think of it like film—you have a piece of film which you are going to edit to another piece of film. You have a choice: join the film to another piece of film and make the entire edit longer (Insert edit) or take a piece of film out of the existing edit, the exact duration of the film you are adding; thus keeping the overall duration the same (Overwrite or Connected edit).

For the moment, let's concentrate on Insert editing.

1   Select a clip within an event; either choose the entire clip or mark a range.

2　Click in the Timeline where you want the edit to take place.

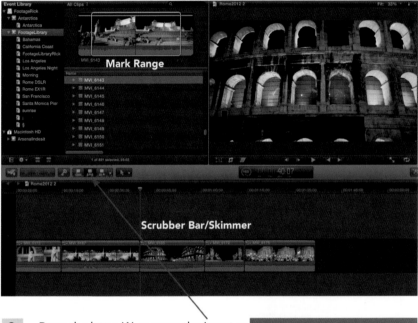

3　Press the letter W or press the Insert symbol on the tool bar.

Notice what takes place: the edit is cut into
the Primary Storyline, and all media after the edit are pushed forward. The overall duration of the Timeline has been made longer.

Above: Before the edit.

Above: After the Insert edit—the duration of the Timeline has been increased.

Every time you do an Insert edit that is how it works—it increases overall duration and pushes the clips further down the Timeline, away from the edit point.

Overwrite Editing

Overwrite editing is the opposite of Insert editing.

Insert editing makes the Timeline longer and pushes everything forward, whereas Overwrite editing does not affect the duration at all. As the name suggests, using this type of edit writes over a portion of the Timeline.

Use the Edit menu to access Overwrite edit, or use the shortcut, which is the letter D.

Edit	View	Mark	Clip	Modify	Shar
Undo					⌘Z
Redo					⇧⌘Z
Cut					⌘X
Copy					**⌘C**
Paste					⌘V
Paste Effects					⌥⌘V
Paste as Connected Clip					⌥V
Reject					⊗
Replace with Gap					⊠
Select All					**⌘A**
Select Clip					**C**
Deselect All					**⇧⌘A**
Connect to Primary Storyline					**Q**
Insert					**W**
Append to Storyline					**E**
Overwrite					**D**
Source Media					▶

1 Select or mark a Range in a clip within an event.

2 Click in the Timeline and position the Skimmer or Playhead where you want the Overwrite edit to take place.

All	⇧1
✓ Video Only	⇧2
Audio Only	⇧3

3 Select to write Video and Audio, Video Only, or Audio Only.

4 Press the letter D or choose Overwrite from the Edit menu.

Overwrite	**D**

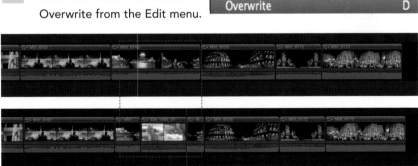

Notice the change to the Timeline where the media has been overwritten, however, the duration of the Timeline remains unchanged.

75

5   Observe the result: a portion of the content in the Primary Storyline
has been written over with media you marked in the Event Viewer.

6   Position the Skimmer in the Timeline and press the space bar to play

Marking a Range in the Timeline

Just as you can mark a range in the clips in the Event Viewer, you can also mark
a range in the Timeline. This lets you define the duration of the content which
can be edited into the Timeline, and this applies to the different types of edits
such as Connected, Insert, and Overwrite.

A range can be marked in the Timeline in three ways:

1   Click on a clip in the Timeline and the entire clip will then be marked as
a Range.

2   Use the letters "i" for in and "o" for out to mark the beginning and end.

3   Alternatively, press the letter R and drag within the Primary Storyline
to set the range. A range can
also be marked within any of
the single Connected Clips.

The duration of the range marked
in the Timeline overrides the range marked in any of the clips in the Event
Browser. This means if you
mark a two-second range
in a clip in an event and
then mark four seconds
in the Timeline, the four-
second duration will apply.
If there aren't four seconds

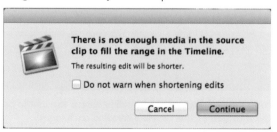

of media available you will get a warning and the choice is then to edit as much media as is available. You can switch off this warning so that this takes place by default each time.

While editing, I constantly bounce between the Timeline and Event Library. Points will be marked in the Timeline, something else marked in the Event Viewer. Press Insert, Overwrite or Add to the Timeline as a Connected Clip. Detach the audio and delete the audio. It all happens very quickly.

You need to get into the flow of editing. Processes and technical functions need to become second nature so you hit the keys already lining up in your mind for the next action, constantly reviewing, trimming, adding to, and deleting sound and picture. The ability to mark a range in the Timeline is a very important enabler for achieving precise results.

Editing Overview

So, we have looked at four types of edits:

1. Append: E
2. Connected: Q
3. Insert: W
4. Overwrite: D

The above ways of editing are all incredibly useful ways of getting content into the Timeline. You can also drag clips directly into the Timeline.

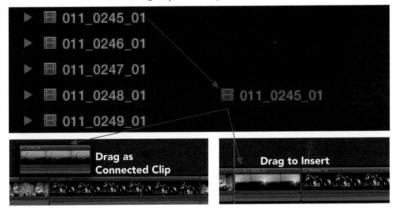

When dragging to the Timeline a Connected edit is performed by dragging above the Primary Storyline; an Insert edit will take place if you drag to the edit point where two clips meet; and a fifth kind of edit is offered if you drag a clip directly on top of a clip in the Primary Storyline—this called a Replace edit.

A contextual menu will appear offering several Replace options. Essentially, a Replace edit means to remove the shot that is already there and replace it with the shot you have chosen. The difference between Replace and Overwrite is that Overwrite works to a defined duration, whereas Replace replaces one shot with another with the duration being defined by the shot you are editing into the Timeline.

You can drag a Connected Clip above or below the Primary Storyline. If the clip is a video clip and you wish for the image to be visible, place the clip above the Primary Storyline. The only likely reason to drag video below the Primary Storyline would be to create a picture-in-picture, or to position a chroma key background (dealt with later). If you are dealing with audio it would make perfect sense to drag this below the Primary Storyline as a Connected Clip.

Mentioned earlier, but worth mentioning again, are the key combinations which make this a quick and simple operation:

- Option + 1:   Video and Audio
- Option + 2:   Video Only
- Option + 3:   Audio Only

Remember—it is not only about getting content into the Timeline, it is about defining exactly what is to be edited: Video and Audio, Video Only, or Audio Only.

It should be obvious that Final Cut Pro X has been designed to be efficient and give you results quickly. Hit a few essential key combinations and in no time you have the content in the Timeline to build your film.

Next you need to access Tools, which give you precision to sculpt your edit into a fine-tuned masterpiece.

Editing Tools

There are seven editing tools in Final Cut Pro X which you need to master:

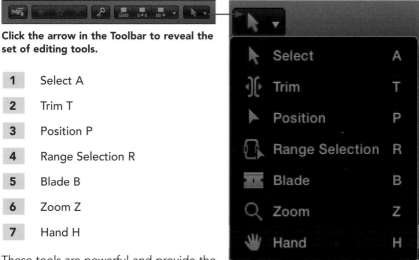

Click the arrow in the Toolbar to reveal the set of editing tools.

1	Select A
2	Trim T
3	Position P
4	Range Selection R
5	Blade B
6	Zoom Z
7	Hand H

These tools are powerful and provide the means to craft your edit. Consider these tools fine-tuning devices in bringing finesse to your edit.

Tools are accessed by selecting the drop-down arrow and then clicking the tool of choice, or you can use the shortcut letters. You can also temporarily select a tool by pressing a letter, for example B for Blade. The tool is active while the letter is held and then returns to the tool which was last selected when you release the letter.

Select A: This is the home tool. Whatever task you perform with any of the other

tools, always return to the Select tool. Simply press the letter A and the tool is then chosen. The Select tool allows you to pick up clips and rearrange them within the Timeline; you can also move Connected Clips; click with this tool on clips in the Timeline and its abilities become clear.

Position P: Press P and the Position tool is selected. This functions similar to the

Select tool with one distinct advantage: whatever you choose and then reposition in the Primary Storyline overwrites that portion of the Timeline. You are free of the restrictions of the Magnetic Timeline; effectively, selecting the Position tool turns the Magnetic Timeline off, while choosing the Select tool A turns it on. With the Position tool selected, wherever you position a clip, or group of clips, will overwrite that area of the Timeline. If no content exists where you reposition the media, then this space becomes inhabited by the media.

Blade B: Press the letter B to select the Blade tool. This lets you slice through a

clip, thereby breaking a clip into smaller chunks. You can then remove content by pressing the delete key, and the Magnetic Timeline will then close the gap with

Below: Highlight a clip or clips in the Timeline.

Below: Delete and clips move to fill the gap.

Below: Hold Shift and press Delete and a gap remains where the media existed.

the remaining clips; or, you can press Shift + Delete and the content is removed and a gap is left. The result is that the duration of the Timeline is unchanged.

Zoom Z: Expanding and contracting the Timeline are critical to editing in Final Cut  Pro X. Sometimes you need to be zoomed right in on the Timeline for fine-detailed work; other times you want to contract the Timeline to get an overview of the edit. Press the letter Z and this selects the Zoom tool. With Skimming switched on and Zoom selected, you can expand the Timeline by clicking with the magnifier. Where you click is the area that is expanded. Hold the Option key, while zooming, and then you can contract the Timeline. Press Shift + Z to condense the Timeline into the available space.

Hand H: Press the letter H and this gives you the ability to grab hold of the entire  Timeline and move it forward or back. No media is moved when using this tool—it is the visual positioning of the Timeline that is affected. I find the Hand tool useful for manually working on specific areas within the Timeline, particularly when the Timeline is expanded larger than what you can view on the screen.

Range Selection: Lets you quickly and easily define a range. Press the letter R and drag  in the Primary Storyline to mark a range, or within any of the Connected Clips. Also used to adjust audio (described later).

It is important to understand that tools are not used in isolation, they are used in combination with each other. Many times I will use the Select tool to juggle a few shots in the Timeline and then switch to the Zoom tool to zoom in close on a specific area. The Position tool would then be used to move a clip to over-write another clip, using the Playhead as the point of reference for where the edit is to occur. This brings us to Snapping.

Snapping toggles on and off using the letter N. It can also be switched on and off by pressing the icon at the far right of the Timeline.

Snapping N toggles on/off.

When skimming through the Timeline, or when dragging the Scrubber Bar, with Snapping switched on the Skimmer/Scrubber Bar will snap to the edit points.

It is as if it magnetically drawn to these—subtle enough that the edit point can be ignored, and strong enough that you can hit the exact point by feeling the hold as you connect to the edit point. This is Snapping.

Very useful. I leave Snapping switched on most of the time. It can also be useful to switch Snapping off so you can freely move through the Timeline without stopping at the edit points.

snapping on.

Snapping off.

Another way to precisely find your way between edit points is by use of the forward and backward arrow keys. Press the up and down arrow keys and you will skip between edit points. Press the horizontal arrow keys and you move forward or backward, one frame at a time. If you hold Shift + Arrow (forward or backward) you skip forward/backward 10 frames with each press.

Up/down arrows move between edit points.

Horizontal arrows move forward a frame at a time; hold Shift + Arrow and move 10 frames at a time.

Between Snapping and the arrow keys I find myself able to precisely located any point in the Timeline, quickly and accurately.

Turning Skimming On and Off

The letter S toggles Skimming on and off. Shift + S toggles audio on/off while skimming.

Skimming   Skimming + Audio

Simply drag across media in the Events Browser or Timeline and the results will be obvious.

Skimming is a great feature for reviewing the footage in your Timeline and clips in the Events Browser, however, there are times when it can get in the way.

Therefore, it can be very useful to hit the letter S and switch Skimming off momentarily, or even for extended periods, while you then use the Scrubber Bar to work your way through the Timeline. Often, while editing, I will hover over the letter S, switching Skimming on/off as needed.

The Concept of Storylines

I've mentioned the Primary Storyline. Just to recap, this is indicated in the Timeline with a dark gray strip; everything else in the Timeline connects or becomes part of the Primary Storyline. The Primary Storyline is where the main action happens—it is where the movie is built. This does not diminish the importance of content which is secondary to the Primary Storyline. The point is that the bulk of editing takes place either in or connected to the Primary Storyline.

Every time you do an Insert edit, an Overwrite, or an Append edit, the result is then added to the Primary Storyline.

When you do a Connect edit (shortcut Q) the result is added to a Secondary Storyline (above or below the Primary Storyline).

Connected Clips are the ones which appear outside the Primary Storyline.

You can also create Secondary Storylines. Simply highlight one or more Connected Clips in the Timeline, and choose Create Storyline.

A Storyline is defined by a darker grey border around the clips. Dissolves can now be added between clips and the Storyline can be moved as a single unit.

Using the Select tool click and move the Secondary Storyline wherever you want it to be placed.

Why would you want to create Secondary Storyline? There are several reasons:

1 A Storyline can be moved as a complete unit. It is much easier to move several clips together as a Storyline than as individual Connected Clips because as a Storyline they all move together. Just as Connected Clips are anchored to the Primary Storyline, so are Secondary Storylines. Secondary Storylines always connect to the Primary Storyline.

2 You can add dissolves or other transitions to the clips inside of a Storyline, whereas it is not possible to add dissolves and other transitions to Connected Clips. Be aware that clips which

are combined into a Storyline will then have the same abilities, in terms of editing techniques that exist in the Primary Storyline.

The rules inside a Secondary Storyline are the same as in the Primary Storyline. The Magnetic Timeline works the same, and each of the tools performs the same function.

If you wish to return clips from being inside a Storyline back into Connected Clips, then highlight and drag the clips out of the Storyline. They will connect to the Primary Storyline where you release them.

If you drag clips out of a Secondary Storyline that have transitions between them, then these will be edited into the Primary Storyline at the closest edit point. The result between dragging clips with or without transitions is different.

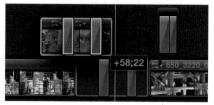

Trimming (in general)

There are several ways to trim media in the Timeline. A basic way to trim is to take the Blade tool, B, cut a clip in the Timeline, and then highlight and delete the media where

you have cut. Working this way, if you press the Delete key the media will be removed and the rest of the Timeline will move to fill the space. If you press Shift + Backspace, then a gap will be left equivalent to the media which has been removed.

You can also trim, using the Select tool, A, by dragging the edit points.

Hover over an edit point and the tools above are revealed: you can drag to extend or reduce clip durations in either direction according to available media.

Hover over an edit point, on either side where two clips meet, and notice that a tool appears with two opposite-facing arrows. There is small filmstrip down the bottom; indicators show which way the tool will operate. If you drag one way you can lengthen or extend the shot you have selected. You can do this from the beginning or end of the shot. The limits to how far you can extend the shot depend on how much media is available on the hard drive.

As you drag to extend or reduce the duration on either side of edit point, the Viewer shows a visual indication of the outgoing and incoming frame.

Providing you have switched on Show

Timeline: ☑ Show detailed trimming feedback

Detailed Trimming Feedback in Preferences, a twin monitor display in the Viewer will visually show the changing edit point.

These two methods enable you to trim in a primitive way: you can slice with the blade, or you can drag the end or beginning point of an edit to lengthen or shorten a shot. These techniques are basic and effective.

For more refined editing, you need to access the Trim tool.

Working with the Trim Tool

Press the letter T to select the Trim tool. This gives you more controls with which to work. With this tool you can perform Roll, Slip, and Slide edits.

Roll edits: Press T to select the Trim tool. Click at an edit point between two clips. Drag the Trim tool from side to side and you see the edit point can be rolled in either direction according to available media. An indicator will show in seconds and frames changes to shot duration. When rolling edits the shot is extended on one side and simultaneously reduced on the other side.

Press T to select the Trim tool.

The edit can be rolled left or right according to available media.

If you have detached audio from video it will be clear how useful this is.

Above: Video has been rolled to the right of the audio, creating a split edit. This provides an effective way to offset video and audio.

You can conveniently roll an edit point without affecting the duration of the Timeline. Audio, if detached from video, is unaffected by Roll editing.

Outgoing media | **Incoming media**

As you trim the results are reflected in the viewer.

As you trim, the Viewer will show the outgoing and incoming frames of the edit (provided you have switched on Show Detailed Trimming Feedback in Preferences). This applies to all functions in Trim mode.

Slip edits: A Slip edit affects the portion of the clip which exists in the Timeline. While slipping the edit, adjusting the start and end point, you draw on the original media, which needs to be longer than the portion included in the Timeline for this type of edit to work. You adjust the clip within the confines of the existing duration.

Press T to choose the Trim Tool. Place your cursor in the center of a clip and drag the clip in either direction within the Timeline. According to available media, the clip content will then be adjusted; as you drag a visual display is shown of the outgoing and incoming

Press T and click in the center of the clip. | **Detailed trimming feedback is displayed as you drag.**

Drag right or left to move the media within the confines of clip duration.

frames (you need to make sure you have Show Detailed Trimming Feedback selected in Preferences).

Slide Edits

Press the Option key with the Trim tool selected and click in the center of a clip in the Timeline. You can move the selected clip in the Timeline left or right, extending or reducing those clips on

Press T and the Trim tool appears as above.

Press T and hold down the Option key to be able to perform Slide edits.

either side of the edit, at the same time maintaining the duration of the edit you are moving. This gives you the means to reposition a clip within those on either side of it. The result is the clip you slide will eat into the clip on one side and extend the media from the other.

Clip in original position.

Drag to the left—notice the duration of the clip is unchanged, however, the clip on the left has been made shorter while the clip on the right has been made longer.

Drag to the right—the clip to the left is extended. The red indicates all available media has been used.

Note: This edit relies on surplus media on drive to be available from the clips on either side of the edit. If the Slide edit doesn't work, reduce the length of the clips on either side of the clip you are sliding and this will create available media to work with.

It may not be immediately clear how useful all these trimming methods are. Let me say, without doubt, if you only use one of the techniques described above, learn how to perform Roll edits. This is as

Video has been positioned separate to audio.

simple as pressing T to select the Trim tool, and then dragging the edit point to a new position. One side of the edit is extended while the edit on the opposite side is made shorter. I think of it as being like a giant film reel releasing film on one side and winding it onto the take-up spool on the opposite side. This lets you precisely adjust edit points while watching the visual feedback to show incoming and outgoing points. Furthermore, if you are working with audio separated from video, you can roll the edits for video without affecting the audio, which lets you do all sorts of magic in the editing.

The Precision Editor

This is a fantastic device which lets you quickly view available media and then adjust the clips on either side of the edit point. It is used for fine-tuning your edits.

1   Press A for the Select tool.

2   Double-click on an edit point in the Timeline.

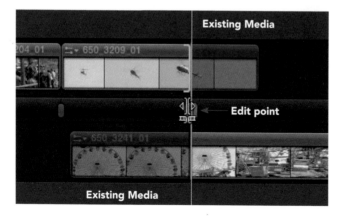

The Precision Editor will now open, and you can see the existing media beyond the edit point, on either side, as being darkened. This media is referred to as handles. It exists on the hard drive and you can draw on this media to extend the edit if you wish.

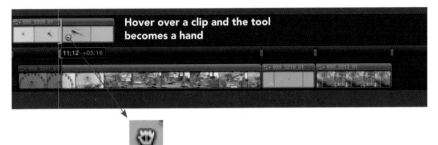

3   If you hover your cursor over one of the clips within the Precision Editor, the icon becomes a hand. You can use the hand to adjust the edit point by dragging. Note: This does affect the duration of the Timeline.

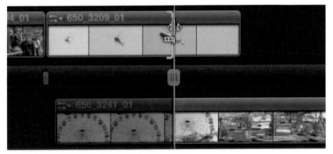

4   If you click on the edit point you can move the media by clicking or dragging to extend or reduce. Again, this will affect the duration of the edit.

5   You can also drag the center indicator and this will adjust the edit point without affecting the duration, essentially performing the same function as a Roll edit.

Note: If you separate video and audio, then you can move the edit point as described in point 5 and audio will remain unaffected.

In summary, within the Precision Editor you have three separate modes with which to fine tune your edit:

1 Use the hand to extend or reduce the media.

Hand

2 Click the media and extend as a range.

Click Media

3 Move the center indicator to perform the same function as a Roll edit.

Center Indicator

Experiment with these methods and it will become clear what the uses are.

To close a clip back to the normal collapsed-state, choose the Close Precision Editor button (bottom right of the Timeline) or double-click the Select tool A on the edit point and the Precision Editor disappears.

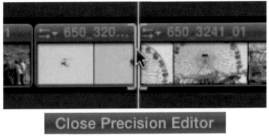

Trimming While Playing Back in the Timeline

One final way to trim media, this time while playing back in the Timeline. You can trim a clip which is stationary or "on the fly" while playing back your edit.

- Option +]:   Trim end of current clip.
- Option + [:   Trim beginning of current clip.

Press Option +]. The trim will take place where the Playhead is positioned. Note the difference in the Timeline below. The media forward of the trim point moves to close the gap.

Media moves back to close the gap.

Press Option + [. The trim will take place where the Scrubber Bar is positioned. Media preceding the Scrubber Bar moves forward to close the gap and the duration of the Timeline is reduced.

————————————→ Media moves forward to close the gap.

By hitting the above key combinations, media is then cut from the end or the beginning of the clip where you are currently positioned. Media in the Timeline moves to close the gap and the duration of the Timeline is affected.

If you have audio separated from video, then different rules apply:

- Option +]:   Video is trimmed, audio is not (audio detached).
- Option + [:   Video is trimmed, audio is not (audio detached).

Option +]. Video is trimmed, audio is not (above).

Media moves back to close the gap and note, below, the audio from the trimmed clip continues beyond the trimmed video.

Option + [. Video is trimmed, audio is not.

Note: The audio now precedes the trim point.

Retiming

Retiming is the word used in Final Cut Pro to describe fast or slow motion.

The controls for slow retiming read Slow 50%, 25%, and 10%, and the Fast controls are for 2x, 4x, 8x, and 20x. Don't be deceived that these are limiting— you can have any speed you want!

Slow	▶	
Fast	▶	2x
Normal 100%	⇧N	4x
Hold	⇧H	8x
		20x
Reverse Clip		
Reset Speed	⌥⌘R	

1 Highlight the clip you wish to adjust.

2 Choose the Retiming menu from the Toolbar. Apply the Slow or Fast setting of your choice.

3 Observe in the Timeline that a color indicator has been applied showing the speed as a percentage. The color blue is used to represent fast motion; orange for slow motion.

▶	50%
	25%
	10%

Drag the right end of the Retiming slider and the indicator will show precise speed changes as you drag. You can adjust the speed to the exact duration you require.

If you wish to reset back to 100% click the speed controls in the center of the clip and set to normal 100%.

Slow	▶
Fast	▶
Normal (100%)	

Or choose Reset Speed from the drop-down menu under the Speed Control icon.

For best-quality slow motion choose the Modify menu, choose Retime, Video Quality, Optical Flow. This is very simple to achieve and is accessed through the Retiming controls, or under the Modify menu at the top of the Final Cut Pro X interface.

Rendering will take longer with Optical Flow switched on but the payback in terms of quality is worth it.

You can also choose to Ramp the speed which means the speed will vary incrementally from 100% to 0% or vice versa. Experiment with the controls as there is a lot on offer to work with.

Create a Freeze Frame

This is easy and is found in the
Retime Controls.

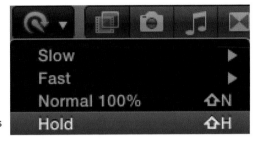

1 Click on a clip in the
Timeline and park the
Playhead on the frame
you wish to freeze. Press
the Retime button.

2 Choose Hold.

3 Zoom in on the Timeline to reveal the area where the freeze now exists.

4 Drag the right end to extend the freeze to the desired length.

You can then use the Blade to cut the freeze into smaller pieces and reposition
as you wish.

Setting Clip Durations

You can easily change the duration of any of the shots
in the Timeline.

1 Click to select a shot in the Timeline.

2 Choose the Modify menu and scroll to Change
Duration (Control D).

3 Notice the center of the Toolbar is
lit up in blue showing the current
duration.

95

4 Type a new duration, for example for 5 seconds, type 500 followed by the Return key.

The new duration is applied to the clip. If you are making the duration shorter this will be applied, however, the maximum amount you can extend a clip is the amount of media that exists on the hard drive.

Setting the duration of the clip is versatile in that it does what it says, which is to set a clip to a predetermined duration; it also offers a quick way to check the duration of any clip in the Timeline. Just highlight a clip, press Control + D, and the duration is displayed in front of you.

Solo Clips

When the Timeline gets busy and crowded with a lot going on, it can be incredibly useful to only listen to the audio from a specific clip or a few select clips and to mute everything else.

Solo button toggles on/off.

This is easily achieved by highlighting a clip or several clips and pressing the Solo button. This is located top right of the Timeline interface, and appears as an icon of the letter S wearing headphones (shortcut Option + S).

1 Highlight the clip you wish to solo.

2 Press the Solo button.

Yellow on. Grey off.

When a clip is solo you will only hear the audio of that clip and all the other clips are silent. This is indicated visually; all the other clips are grayed out.

In the example above three clips are solo, with the silent clips being grayed out.

Soloing can be particularly useful when working with multiple sound elements. You may have voice over, sound effects, and music. To combine all these elements you need to be able to adjust these independently to create a complete soundtrack, with cohesive elements that don't fight against each other. When creating the audio soundtrack soloing is a powerful means to isolate a particular part of the soundtrack and adjust as needed.

Disable Clips

You can also disable clips, which means to kill the audio and video from a particular clip or clips.

1 Using the Select A tool highlight a clip or group of clips in the Timeline.

2 Choose the Clip menu and scroll to Disable or press the letter V.

Clip	Modify	Share	Window
Create Storyline			⌘G
Synchronize Clips			⌥⌘G
Open in Timeline			
Disable			**V**

Highlight clip or clips in Timeline

Press the letter V to disable the clip or clips

Separate video & audio - video disabled

Separate video & audio - audio disabled

The clip or clips you have disabled remain in the Timeline, however they cannot be seen or heard.

It is very easy and quick to at any point press the letter V and disable a clip and then press V to enable it again. When you are working with multiple layers this can be very useful.

Compound Clips

We've covered several concepts so far: the Events Library, Keywording, Connected Clips, and Primary and Secondary Storylines. Now, it is time for one more concept: Compound Clips.

Essentially, a Compound Clip is several clips, or even an entire Timeline of media, collapsed down into a single clip. The single clip is the Compound Clip.

Compound Clips can be expanded so that you can go back inside at the media which makes up the Compound Clip, and, if you wish, you can lose the Compound Clip entirely and return to the original expanded state of the media.

To create a Compound Clip:

1   Highlight the clips in the Timeline which you wish to combine into a single clip.

Highlight clips

2   Choose New Compound Clip from the File menu at the top of the interface or press the shortcut, Option + G.

Observe the result, which is a single clip in the Timeline of the duration of all the highlighted clips which previously existed.

File	Edit	View	Mark	Clip	M
New Project...					⌘N
Project Properties...					⌘J
New Event					⌥N
New Keyword Collection					⇧⌘K
New Folder					⇧⌘N
New Smart Collection					⌥⌘N
New Compound Clip...					⌥G

Compound Clip

Original clips

Double-click anywhere on the Compound Clip and you can see the individual clips; these can be adjusted, recut, and changed as you wish, and the changes are then reflected when playing back the Compound Clip.

To return to the Timeline, with the Compound Clip in position, click the arrow back button located top left of the Timeline.

To get rid of a Compound Clip so that the original, expanded media appears in the Timeline, highlight the Compound Clip and choose Break Apart Clip Items from the Clip menu (shortcut Command +

Clip	Modify	Share	Window
Create Storyline			⌘G
Synchronize Clips			⌥⌘G
Open in Timeline			
Audition			▶
Reveal in Event Browser			⇧F
Show Video Animation			^V
Show Audio Animation			^A
Solo Animation			^⇧V
Show Precision Editor			^E
Expand Audio / Video			^S
Clear Audio/Video Split			
Detach Audio			^⇧S
Break Apart Clip Items			⇧⌘G

Shift + G). This will return you to the edited clips and the Compound Clip will no longer be visible.

The huge advantage of working with Compound Clips is you can take a very busy, sophisticated edit, and reduce its size so that it is manageable. Too much information in the Timeline can be unwieldy to work with—to collapse it can make life simpler. A warning: don't overuse Compound Clips and don't put Compound Clips inside of Compound Clips. This has been known to stress out the computer!

Whizzing around the Timeline Using Markers

It can be useful to use Markers to pinpoint a location to which you can quickly return. A Marker can be left as a signpost anywhere in the Timeline, they can be color coded, and notes can be assigned to them.

1   Park the Skimmer anywhere in Timeline and press the letter M. This will leave a marker on the clip where you were positioned in the Timeline.

2   Go somewhere else in the Timeline and again press the letter M.

3   One more time repeat the process.

Markers in blue

You should now have the Timeline with three separate Markers. You can move between the markers by pressing the following key combinations:

- Control + '   Jump forward to next marker.
- Control + ;   Jump backward to previous marker.

This is incredibly useful—it means at any time you can jump to a predetermined point in the Timeline. It is very simple to quickly move backwards or forwards.

Markers serve more purposes than simply to move around in the Timeline.

When setting a marker, instead of pressing M, press the letter M twice in quick succession. A dialog box will open, giving you the choice to enter details for the marker.

If you press Make to Do Item the marker will then visually stand out in the color red. This is easy to spot, even on a very busy Timeline.

To do item in red.

If you control-click on a Marker you get options to choose from. Notably, you can cut a marker, to get rid of it, or mark as a To Do Item. Once Completed the Marker color changes to green. There is also an option to Delete a Marker.

Cut Marker
Copy Marker

Modify Marker
✓ To Do
Completed

Delete Marker

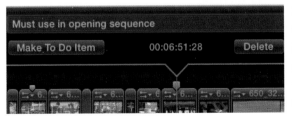

If you press Shift + M while positioned on a Marker, or double-click a Marker, this will reveal the notes which have been entered.

I think of markers as being like pegs or beacons—you can home in very quickly exactly where you want to be.

Cut, Copy, and Paste

Any of the media in the Timeline can be cut, copied, or pasted, just like using a word processor. Clips can be copied and pasted within a project or between different projects.

- Command + X: Cut
- Command + C: Copy
- Command + V: Paste
- Option + V: Paste as Connected Clip

1   Highlight any clip or clips you wish to cut or copy.

2   Press Command + X to cut the clips or Command + C to copy the clips.

3   Reposition the Skimmer or click to position the Scrubber Bar and press Command + V. The media will then be pasted at the place you have decided.

4   If you wish to Paste as a Connected Clip then type Option + V. This clip is then positioned above for video, or below for audio.

Connected Clip pasted into the Timeline

Note: When cutting from the Primary Storyline the clips to the right will move and close any gaps which have been created (the Timeline will be made shorter); when pasting into the Timeline the result is that of an Insert edit: any media after the Insert will be shunted down the Timeline to the right, and the Timeline will therefore increase in length. When pasting as Connected Clips the duration of the Timeline will remain unaffected.

Duplicating Projects

When I have done a load of work and wish to protect it I often duplicate the project.

1 Go to the Project Library.

2 Highlight the project you wish to duplicate.

3 Control-click and choose Duplicate Project.

4 Choose the option Duplicate Project (shortcut Command + D). Alternatively choose File, Duplicate Project.

You will be greeted with a window with three options:

1 Duplicate Project Only: This literally means to duplicate the project and not the media. Use this when duplicating a project from the same drive to the same drive. I often use this to manually save a version to which I will give a date and time in case I wish to return to an earlier edit. If you choose not to include render files you will find the process is instant. I then rename the project accordingly.

2   Duplicate Project and Referenced Events: This means to duplicate everything that is associated with the project. All the media, events, audio, graphics, and still images will be copied to the location you specify. I use this most often for archiving a project to a separate hard drive. Therefore, I select the hard drive to which I want to copy the project and media.

3   Duplicate Project and Used Clips Only: This is another very useful way to archive a project, however be aware that only media used in the edit is copied. Clips not used in the edit will not be copied.

Drag projects from one hard drive to another to duplicate.

If you wish to duplicate a project from one hard drive to another a quick and easy way is to drag the project from its current location and drop it onto the hard drive where it is to be copied. This will then open the Duplicate Project window and you can choose from the settings.

These are powerful media management capabilities which enable you to back up projects, copy the project and media to a separate hard drive which can then be plugged into different Macs, or to quickly create a copy of a project which you may choose to time stamp so you can then return to an earlier version at any point.

Locating Clips in the Event Library or on the Hard Drive

When I worked in online edit suites, filled with open-reel tape machines, spinning in sync, with an edit controller and vision mixer to make it all happen, we used to do a fair bit of match frame editing. This meant you would mark the "in" point on a source tape, and the exact frame would be spooled to on the original master tape. It was the quickest way to locate the original media and also very useful in effects creation.

In Final Cut Pro X, you have two facilities to help you track down media and to do a match frame edit if you wish. Control-click any clip in the Timeline and choose one of the following:

1 Reveal in Event Browser will show the clip in the Event where it is located, being matched to the frame you choose in the Timeline.

The clip in the Timeline (below) is matched to in the Event Browser.

2 Reveal in Finder will show the clip in the location where it exists on the hard drive.

Both of the above are incredibly useful for tracking down your media within the project or on the drive, and enabling you to match the frame edit if you need to.

Reveal All the Clips Used in Your Project

If you want to see a quick overview of the media you
have used in your project, meaning a complete listing of
all the clips, then click the lower left of the Timeline on
the Timeline Index icon—the list of clips will now appear in front of you.

You can use the arrows to move up or down or click any of the clips to show in
the Viewer; note as you click the selected clip is then highlighted in the Timeline.

Control-click the clip in the Timeline and select Reveal in the Event Browser to
locate and/or match a frame to a clip (shortcut Shift +F).

Auditioning

Auditioning gives you the means to quickly switch between different shots in
the Timeline. I think of it as being like a giant carousel switching sources in real
time though a giant projector…

1 Highlight a clip or range in the Timeline.

2 Highlight a clip or clips in the Event Browser.

3   Drag the clips from the Event Browser on top of the clip in the Timeline wherever you choose and then select Add to Audition.

Alternatively, choose from the Clip menu at the top of the interface.

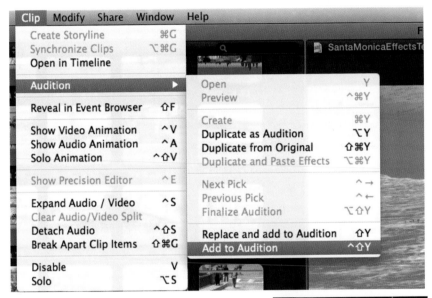

Notice a new spotlight icon appears to the left top of the clip to show that clips are ready to be Auditioned.

4   Press the letter Y to open the audition, or control-click on the clip and select this command.

The Audition window will open in front of you. Position the Playhead and press

the space bar to play.

Press Control + forward/back arrows to skip through the shots you have lined up in the Audition window.

When you find a shot you want included in the edit, press Done and the clip will drop into place.

If you want to add another clip or clips to the audition choose Add to Audition and continue the process. You can remove a clip from the Audition by selecting it and pressing the Delete key.

Rendering

Rendering is the process which takes place to build the frames of your movie for output. Rendering is not always required, however, when footage is manipulated and changed, then it does need to be rendered, not necessarily to play back, but for final output. Changes such as color correction, opacity changes, retiming, and stretching or cropping of the image or adding titles all require rendering.

Modify	Share	Window	Help

Analyze and Fix...

Adjust Content Created Date and T

Balance Color
Match Color...

Auto Enhance Audio
Match Audio...
Volume

Add Keyframe to Selected Effect in

Change Duration...
Retime

Apply Custom Name

Assign Roles
Edit Roles...

Render All
Render Selection

Whenever you see an orange bar at the top of the Timeline this means that the portion media needs to be rendered.

If you have Background Render switched on in Preferences, then rendering will begin within a few seconds. Final Cut waits for a lull in activity and then rendering kicks in…

If you have Background switched off then you can manually start the render process by choosing the Modify menu and scrolling to:

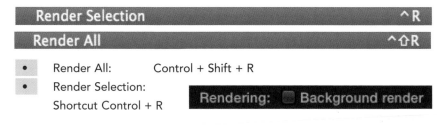

| Render Selection | ^R |
| Render All | ^⇧R |

- Render All: Control + Shift + R
- Render Selection:
  Shortcut Control + R

Much of the time I work with Background Render switched off in Preferences and manually render when I choose. This is useful for two reasons: (1) rendered files take up drive space, so you aren't generating unnecessary files, the only files generated are those you choose to create; and (2) having Background Render fire up every time you stop for a few seconds can be distracting.

Putting it all Together

Just remember editing isn't one thing, it's everything; it is how you use the tools in combination with each other which will let you fly through the editing process and turn out the results.

There is still a huge amount to explore with Final Cut Pro X. For the moment, absorb the key concepts of how to organize media, how to get footage edited into the Timeline, and how to make it work in terms of pace and structure. Next we move on to audio production, where you make your production sound as good as it looks.

Sound Mixing

Even though this is a separate chapter in the book, I want to make the point that sound mixing is not necessarily something which happens separate from the rest of the editing. I will mix my sound as I cut picture. Sometimes, if I have the time, I'll spend more time on the audio, which may well be after the picture edit is complete. Sometimes, when there is no time, I may call on some of the audio-functionality built into Final Cut Pro X to sort out any of the differences in levels between clips.

I'm old school. I like manual control over my audio so I know what is going on. However, I'm also on the cutting edge. I like to make use of new technology to better the end product and to make my life easier. Final Cut Pro X has some nice facilities to help you create a seamless audio mix.

The basics which one must run through, in terms of audio production, for producing any video or film include the following processes: (i) adjust audio levels, (ii) add sound fades, (iii) mix the sound to be music, narration, sound effects, or whatever, (iv) balance any peaks or falls in the sound and monitor the sound and check the output level, (v) work with stereo pairs, (vi) build multiple layers of audio and solo/disable audio at will, (vii) synchronize audio, where a master record needs one or more cameras to be synced together, (viii) keyframe audio fades, and (ix) pan tracks.

That's enough for now. There could be more work beyond this, but the list above is pretty comprehensive in terms of the general tasks which need to be fulfilled.

Back to Basics

Just a reminder, clips inside Final Cut Pro X appear as video and audio combined in the same clip. By running through the options in Clip Appearance you can view only the audio information if you choose, or you have the option to show video thumbnails and audio combined.

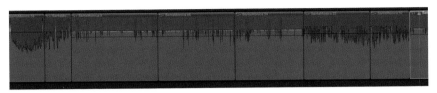

For the purposes of mixing sound, it can be useful to make the audio as large as possible by adjusting the clip height.

Double-click the audio to separate visually.

You can view separate video and audio by double-clicking the audio track to visually separate the two.

If you want to separate video and audio so that they are truly separate, highlight a clip and choose Detach Audio from the Clip menu.

Clip	Modify	Share	Window
Create Storyline			⌘G
Synchronize Clips			⌥⌘G
Open in Timeline			
Audition			▶
Reveal in Event Browser			⇧F
Show Video Animation			^V
Show Audio Animation			^A
Solo Animation			^⇧V
Show Precision Editor			^E
Expand Audio / Video			^S
Clear Audio/Video Split			
Detach Audio			^⇧S
Break Apart Clip Items			⇧⌘G

The audio then becomes a Connected Clip to the video. Therefore, if the video is moved, the audio, which is connected to the video, will move with it. However, you also have the power to move the audio

Audio moved separate to video.

separate from the video just by
clicking on it and dragging. If you

New Compound Clip...   ⌥G

wish to combine video and audio into a single clip, then highlight the elements
and choose Compound Clip from the File menu.

For those who have used other editors, the familiar way to work with audio is
to have two tracks to access. Most professional cameras record to two separate
audio tracks, with separate XLR inputs; some even allow for four separate tracks.

It is important to be able to access those tracks inside of Final Cut Pro X.

It is as simple as control-
clicking on the audio and
selecting Open in Timeline.

New Compound Clip...   ⌥G
Open in Timeline

The twin tracks will then be revealed ready for you to access.

Adjust the Audio Level within a Clip

The basic job of adjusting audio levels from clip to clip is as simple as can be in
Final Cut Pro X.

Make sure you have Clip Appearance set so that you can clearly see the audio
waveforms. When mixing audio, I will often set the display to only show the
audio waveform (the first choice in Clip Appearance).

Switch on the
audio meters so
you can visually
see the changes
in the audio level.

**Above: Click to reveal audio meters to the right
of the Timeline.**

Audio meters.

Press the Audio Meters icon in the Dashboard to show or hide the meters.

Green during playback shows the audio is good, yellow shows you are peaking, and red shows you are over-peaking and risk distortion.

The basic rule is don't hit the red on the meters. I let my audio run at between –12 and –6 dB.

If you wish to make the audio display even larger, drag the Clip Height slider to increase or decrease the size.

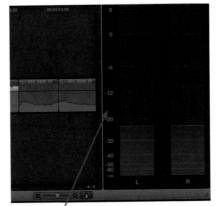

Drag where the Timeline meets the audio meters to extend the width.

Adjusting audio levels within a clip is simple:

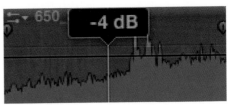

1. Use the Select A tool and drag the black line in the center of the clip up or down.

An indicator will show in dB how much you raise or lower the audio.

2. You will notice indicators in audio clips in the Timeline. Drag the black line in the clip up, raising the volume; when you release, the

indicators will show yellow or red to indicate over-peaking. Adjust so the absolute peaks hit the yellow but not the red.

3. Check the playback on the audio meters to confirm these are correct.

You can also raise the audio level in small increments, on the fly during playback, by pressing **Control +** (volume up) or **Control –** (volume down). Simply highlight the clip and adjust the level as you listen to the result, again watching the audio meters as well as the clip indicators.

Fading Audio

The audio fade has been with us forever and is the primary way of smoothing out bumps in the audio so you can create a montage of sound which blends seamlessly together. Sometimes you want an audio cut, sometimes you want a fade. A fade provides a gentle transition.

The audio can be faded very easily from the head or the tail:

1   Position your curser over a clip in the Timeline.

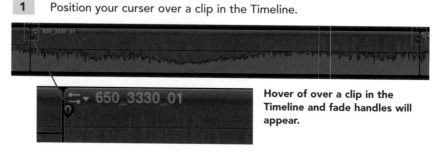

Hover of over a clip in the Timeline and fade handles will appear.

2   Hover your curser over a clip in the Timeline. Look to the ends of the clip and notice at the beginning or end of the clip are handles, represented by a small dot.

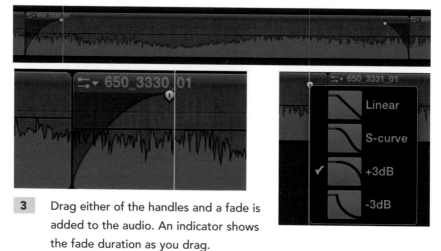

3   Drag either of the handles and a fade is added to the audio. An indicator shows the fade duration as you drag.

If you control-click on the handle at the beginning or end of the shot, you are given options to change the shape of the fade. Experiment with these and listen to the result and choose that which is most suitable.

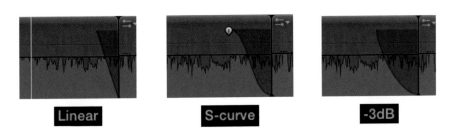

Linear — S-curve — -3dB

Fading Audio Using the Range Tool

You can also fade the audio within a clip using the Range Tool R. This provides an incredibly useful means to making fine adjustments to the audio within a single clip.

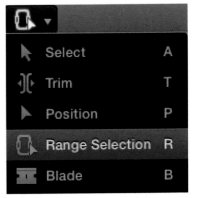

▶ Select	A
◀▶ Trim	T
▶ Position	P
◻ Range Selection	R
◼ Blade	B

1 Press the letter R to select the Range tool or choose the drop-down menu in the Toolbar.

2 Click with the Range tool and drag within a clip in the Timeline to define the area you wish to adjust.

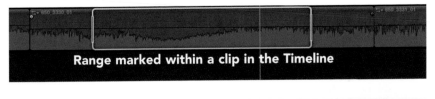

Range marked within a clip in the Timeline

3 Once you have marked the range, click the black line in the center of the clip and drag this up to increase the audio level

Drag the black line up or down

or drag down to reduce. An indicator will show the level of increase or decrease in dB as you drag. The result is that a fade is added to the beginning and end of the range. You can see the fade represented visually; furthermore, you can adjust the fade points by dragging.

117

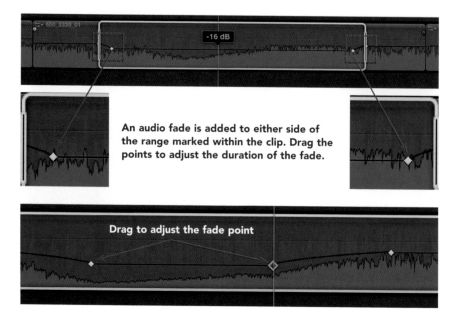

An audio fade is added to either side of the range marked within the clip. Drag the points to adjust the duration of the fade.

Drag to adjust the fade point

This method provides an amazingly quick way to ramp up or dip down the audio as needed.

Keyframing Audio

To keyframe means to change over time. You can plot points within the audio of a clip and make adjustments as you wish by dragging the fade points.

1   Hold down the Option key and click the black line within a clip. Notice a dot will be added to represent a fade handle.

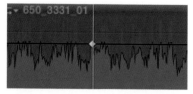

Control + Click the black line in the center of the clip to add audio Keyframes

Repeat the process. Option and click to add as many points as you wish.

2 Grab any of the fade handles and drag to adjust. You will visually see the fades plotted within the clip with an indicator showing the increase or decrease in dB.

3 Listen to hear the result, and watch the audio meters to confirm you don't over-modulate.

To remove any of the fade points you have added, simply click the fade point, which will then turn orange. Press Delete on your keyboard and the small dot will then disappear.

Adding Audio Mixes

Along with the audio fade there is the audio mix, which is an overlapping fade between the two audio sources. This is one of the most used tools for creating a smooth-sounding mix. A quick audio fade, two or three frames, can be used to remove pops and clean up edits, whereas a longer audio fade can be used to introduce sounds to the mix so that nothing is jarring. When mixing audio, most of the time, the goal is not to alert the viewer to the mix; rather, it should be unnoticeable. Using audio fades can help us achieve this.

We can mix between two audio sources. To do this, we need at least two clips edited side-by-side in the Timeline with overlap, meaning more media must exist on the hard drive to draw upon to produce the fade. You can actually check available media by opening the Precision Editor. Double-click the edit point and available media, beyond that  which has been used, appears transparent. Note: You cannot detach audio once the Precision Editor is open. This needs to be done first.

1   Make sure you have two clips cut together with audio detached.

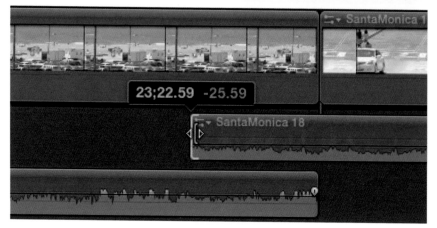

2   With the Select A tool chosen, drag the audio from one of the clips toward the clip next to it. The clip which you are dragging toward will then shunt out of the way (it is important that the Select A tool is being used!).

3 Drag the Fade Handles for the incoming and outgoing clips. Visual indicators show the duration of the fade as you drag. You can therefore quite easily plot an 8-frame or 12-frame audio fade. For precise control, expand the Timeline using the Zoom tool, Z; you can zoom right down to the subframe level if you wish! Play back and listen to confirm the result is what you want. You may also wish to Roll the edit to move the video cut to follow or precede the audio transition.

Working with Dual Track Audio

It was mentioned earlier that clips with twin audio tracks or more can be hidden within a single combined track. These audio tracks can be accessed by control-clicking on a clip and selecting Open in Timeline.

The Open in Timeline command can be accessed either directly inside the Timeline, or in the Events Browser by control-clicking any of the clips.

You can choose the command Open in Timeline regardless of whether audio is separate from video or combined with video.

The clip opens up to reveal the two separate audio tracks and you can edit these as you wish, as separate tracks—razor blading, keyframing the mix, and adjusting however you wish.

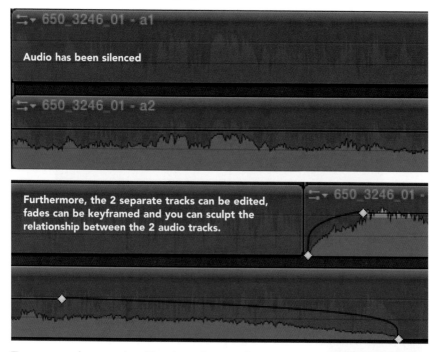

Many times camera rushes will be recorded with master audio on one track and the camera mic on another; the task for the

editor will be to remove the inferior camera mic audio. This is where the Open in Timeline command becomes tremendously useful. Drag the audio to 0 dB to silence the audio, or you can highlight and delete the track.

To return to the complete Timeline of your edit, press the back arrow at the top left of the Timeline.

Changes in the audio mix are then reflected in the mix on playback.

Break Apart Clip Items

Another way to reveal the separate audio tracks is to choose the command Break Apart Clip Items. This will Detach audio from video and break the audio into separate tracks.

I have encountered situations where Open in Timeline has worked when Break Apart Clip Items has not, so take your choice and use which method works best for you.

You can select multiple clips in the Timeline and then select Break Apart Clip Items and the dual tracks are then available to access for each of the clips.

Clip	Modify	Share	Window
Create Storyline			⌘G
Synchronize Clips			⌥⌘G
Open in Timeline			
Audition			▶
Reveal in Event Browser			⇧F
Show Video Animation			^V
Show Audio Animation			^A
Solo Animation			^⇧V
Show Precision Editor			^E
Expand Audio / Video			^S
Clear Audio/Video Split			
Detach Audio			^⇧S
Break Apart Clip Items			⇧⌘G
Disable			V
Solo			⌥S

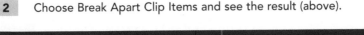

1   Highlight clips in Timeline (above).

2   Choose Break Apart Clip Items and see the result (above).

3   You can then fade, pan, and edit the audio as you wish.

123

Relationship of the Inspector to Audio Output

A key part of the interface which we have barely touched upon so far is the Inspector.

The Inspector can be accessed by pressing the "i" button (right of the interface). The shortcut Command + 4 will toggle the Inspector on or off.

The Inspector is a place where you can access many of the controls for editing, audio editing, effects production, and titling. The Inspector reacts to that which you have selected; therefore, click the audio of a clip and Inspector displays the audio properties and choices. Choose the video and you can access controls which affect the video. Once we get onto effects production, you will see controls and parameters specific to this area.

Click the audio of a clip in the Timeline and open up the Inspector window; press the Inspector icon on the interface or choose Command + F4.

Setting Audio Pan Controls

The first video editing I ever did was working in a two-machine Betacam suite. Two-tape machines wired up, a player, and a recorder with an edit controller to control each of the machines. There is a preview button and a record button bang in the center. This was standard Beta, analogue half-inch tape, before Beta SP and way before DigiBeta hit the scene.

On Betacam, you could work with two tracks of audio: stereo, left or right. You could do a lot with two tracks—music on one, interview on the other, then do a mixdown to add some effects. It was primitive, but it worked, and we knocked out results which were broadcast every night on the six o'clock news, onlined in two-machine suites and fed out to the world.

In that two-machine suite was an audio mixer, so we could ride the levels and mix the audio live. At the top of the mixer were pan controls. It had the essential knobs—turn one way and audio could be directed to the left or the right channel, turn the other and you could balance the audio so that the master track fed equally to tracks 1 and 2 on the record machine.

That's what pan controls do. This lets you mix audio evenly so the track you have chosen will play out of both the left and right channels, or, you can choose to direct the sound left or right or anything in between. This is the process by which the editor creates a stereo or mono mix.

It is important to be aware when setting the pan controls in Final Cut Pro X that you can work with audio where video and audio are represented as a single clip or you can work where the video and audio are Detached.

Furthermore, you can choose to work with the clip as a two separate tracks, by using the Open in Timeline command. You can then apply the pan controls to the individual tracks.

To set the audio pan controls in Final Cut Pro X:

1   Click on a clip in the Timeline.

2 Open the Inspector (Command + 4 to toggle on and off).

3 Click the second tab, Audio.

4 You can now choose a pan mode.

5 Choose Stereo Left/Right.

Video	Audio	Info

Volume and Pan

Volume: ———

Pan Mode: None ▼

Audio   Info

🔊 650_3332_01 - a1   00:00:03;28

Effects   ↩

Volume and Pan   ↩

Volume: ———————————   0

Pan Mode: Stereo Left/Right ▼   ▼

Pan Amount:

	None
	Default
	✓ Stereo Left/Right

Audio Enhancemen   Create Space

Dialogue

Equalization: Music

Audio Analysis: Ambience

Circle

Channel Configurat   Rotate

Back to Front

Channels: Left Surround to Right Front

Right Surround to Left Front

---

6 Use the slider to adjust the pan amount. Using this you can adjust the pan Left/Right and you can hear the result as you pan.

Volume: ————⬧————   -8

Pan Mode: Stereo Left/Right ▼

Pan Amount: ————⬧————   0

Drag the Pan Amount slider one way and you hear the audio out of the left speaker; drag the other way and sound comes from the right. Set the pan control in the middle and sound is distributed equally through both speakers. The result is also reflected on the audio meters (press the Meters icon on the Dashboard in the Toolbar if these are not visible).

Press to reveal audio meters.

7   Be aware adjusting the pan for a single track of stereo audio is very different from adjusting the pan for individual tracks of audio. That is when you use the commands Open in Timeline or Break Apart Clip Items; this will let you access the individual tracks. I like to know the makeup of the audio tracks and much of the time I choose to work with dual audio tracks. I can quickly remove stray audio or camera mic by deleting a track or by silencing the audio. The best audio can then, if I choose, be panned to mono so the sound is equally heard out of the two speakers.

> Volume:
> Pan Mode: Stereo Left/Right ▼
> **Pan left**
> Pan Amount:

> Volume:
> Pan Mode: Stereo Left/Right ▼
> **Centered**
> Pan Amount:

As mentioned earlier, adjusting pan controls was standard practice in edit suites over 20 years ago in broadcast tape suites. It gives you the means to control your audio, to produce a stereo or mono mix, and to get rid of unwanted sound.

> Volume:
> Pan Mode: Stereo Left/Right ▼
> **Pan right**
> Pan Amount:

Switching Audio Tracks On and Off in the Inspector

Audio tracks can be turned on or off in the Inspector simply by checking or unchecking the controls.

 Click on a clip in the Timeline.

2 Look to the Inspector under the Audio tab. Notice at the bottom is an area called Channel Configuration. Here the audio associated with the clip can be worked with a dual mono or stereo. Think of the representation in the Inspector as being a reflection of the audio in the Timeline.

Above: Dual mono representation of the clip in the Timeline.

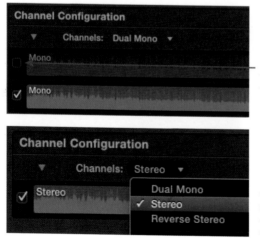

Left: Tracks can be muted by checking or unchecking the box to the left. This presents a quick way to silence the audio.

Left: If the Channel Configuration is changed to stereo, then the result is that one, not two, track is visible in Channel Configuration.

Boosting Audio Levels with the Gain Filter

Many times audio is recorded on location at a lower level than is ideal. This can be fixed in the edit suite by boosting the audio. The means to adjust audio in the Timeline is limited to a maximum of +12 dB. When you need more volume, do the following:

1 Highlight the clip you wish to adjust in the Timeline. If you are working with separate video and audio, then highlight the audio.

2 Open up Video and Audio Effects.

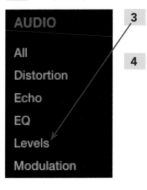

3 Scroll down so you can see the audio choices and click Levels.

4 Locate the Gain filter. You then need to apply this to the clip you have highlighted by double-clicking the Gain icon or by dragging this onto the clip.

The Effects window for audio and video is a pane which shows available effects, separated with video at the top and audio at the bottom.

Note the search dialog box at the bottom of the window. Key in the name of an effect, such as Gain, and the search results will be shown before you.

Once you learn the name of the effects you use most frequently you can then key in the info to find them very quickly.

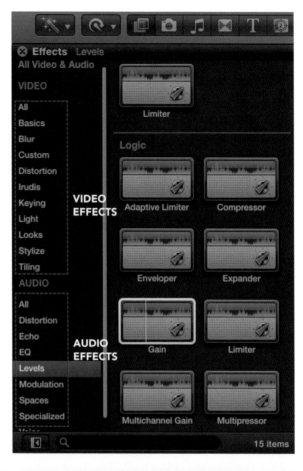

The search results are then displayed before you.

5 Once you have applied the Gain filter to a clip go to the Inspector, look to the audio controls, and under effects is Gain. Click the arrow to reveal adjustable parameters and functionality.

6 Adjust the parameters. You can boost the overall volume considerably and you have other controls, including Pan control, and the ability to mono the track or swap channels.

Drag the slider to increase or decrease the gain. Maximum gain is +24 dB, plus you can increase audio in the Timeline by +12 dB.

Keep an eye on the audio meters, particularly when boosting with Gain, as it is easy to completely over do it.

Using the Gain filter provides a quick way to increase the audio level. If you need even more level, then apply the Gain filter twice or as many times as you need to boost the audio to whatever level is required.

Once the effect is applied you can play your audio and adjust in real time to hear the result.

Above: Two Gain filters have been applied to the same clip.

131

Keyframing Audio Gain

Getting inside the audio and then plotting keyframe points can be achieved by showing Audio Animation.

1   Apply the audio Gain filter to a clip in the Timeline.

2   To the left of the clip in the Timeline click the downward arrow icon and select Show Audio Animation.

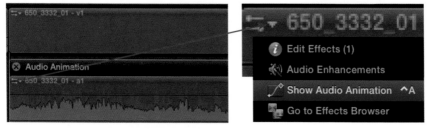

Click and choose Show Audio Animation.

3   A strip is revealed at the base of the audio track. It is here the Keyframe points can be plotted.

4   Position the Skimmer and press Option Click to mark keyframe points.

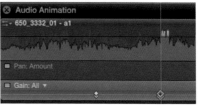

5 Drag the points within the Audio Animation area to raise or lower the gain or make changes to the parameters in the Inspector.

6 To Delete a keyframe in the Animation Editor click and press the delete key.

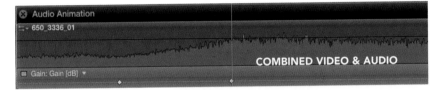

7 Close Audio Animation when you are happy with the result.

Note: The images shown for this section have been for adjusting the audio Gain with Detached audio.

The process with combined video and audio is similar, though be aware that you will be applying Gain changes globally to the stereo or mono tracks. Parameters can be adjusted in the Channel Configuration area of the Inspector.

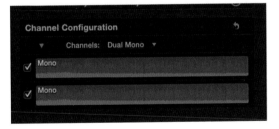

Automated Loudness: Setting Audio Levels Quickly

In general, I'm not a fan of automation, that is, to let Final Cut Pro X take care of tasks which I feel can be better managed manually.

However, there is a fantastic automated control in the Inspector which will boost or reduce the audio level of a clip so that it peaks correctly. You can use this method to sort out the audio levels for individual clips or an entire scene, simply by turning part of the Timeline into a Compound Clip.

1   Highlight the media you wish to work with.

2   Go to the Inspector and select the Audio tab.

3   Choose Audio Enhancements and click the arrow to the right.

Click the arrow to take you into Audio Enhancements.

4   Check the control at the top—Loudness.

The result is that the audio level of the clip is now set to the correct level. You can also adjust Uniformity which affects the overall dynamic range in the audio.

I have used the Audio Analysis to enhance audio many times when rushed, to quickly even out audio levels. As written earlier, take a group of several or many clips and turn these into a Compound Clip. Highlight the Compound Clip, go to the Inspector, and then select the audio controls. Click the arrow to the right of Audio Enhancements and check the box for Loudness.

This function works and it works well. However, beware—if music is in the mix some very strange results can occur, so I avoid using this where music is involved. Furthermore, I firmly believe that the best audio mix is the result of human ears listening and interacting to create a result; not the result of pressing a single button to iron out any audio shifts. Thus, I use this method sparingly. But when you're in a hurry and need to get the job done and out the door really quickly, then you do what needs to be done!

Graphic Equalizer

EQing your audio has always been an essential part of the filmmaking process. Sometimes you need to get rid of hiss, other times the audio is too boomy, so the bass needs to be cut.

The Graphic Equalizer in Final Cut Pro X is easy to access and lets you boost and diminish frequencies by dragging and listening. The results play back in real time.

1 Click the clip in the Timeline you wish to adjust.

2 Go to the audio controls in the Inspector.

3 Go to Audio Enhancements and click the Equalization menu to reveal the choices. You can either leave this on flat, which leaves your audio untouched, or you can choose one of the options.

4 Click the icon to bring up the Graphic Equalizer.

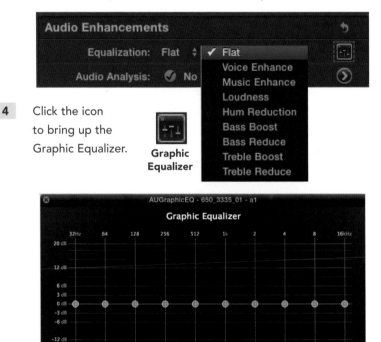

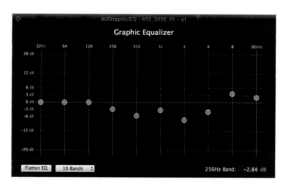

5   Drag the faders to adjust and listen to the result playing back in real time.

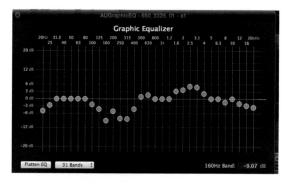

6   For more sophisticated EQing, you can choose a 31-band Graphic Equalizer.

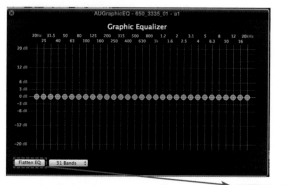

7   You can reset the faders by pressing Flatten EQ.   **Flatten EQ**

EFFECTS

Effects creation is where the action happens. You can combine many elements, composite images, and graphics together, add titles, transitions, and jazz up a production so that it is more than just cuts in a Timeline.

Furthermore, you can treat the images by applying video effects and, if you wish, you have access to a wide variety of prebuilt Templates. Truly remarkable results can be achieved, adjusted, and set according to your needs.

Beyond this is color correction, which offers the ability to sort out white balance issues, tweak the image to warm it up, cool it down, push the black levels, or increase/decrease the whites.

When I started cutting in the late 1980s such power would have been a dream.

Types of Effects

There are five types of effects we are going to be dealing with:

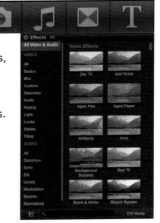

1 Video and audio effects: The effects change the image in terms of color, texture, brightness, and a host of other parameters. Audio too can be manipulated to adjust sound frequencies, level, pitch, and other settings.

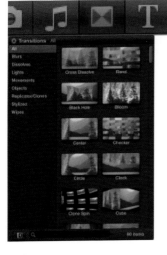

2 Transitions: Transitions are applied between clips. The most common transition, the dissolve, is used in all types of productions from home movies to features films. Other wacky transitions can be drawn upon for impact or to add punch to a video.

3 Text: A tremendous amount of text options are offered within Final Cut Pro X for title creation. Everything from a simple static title, to customized moving titles, lower thirds, and captions can be quickly and easily created and positioned.

4 Generators: This refers to elements available inside Final Cut Pro X such as backgrounds, textures, and other elements to work with.

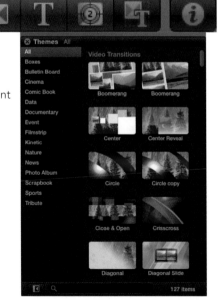

5 Themes: Themes are prebuilt moving backgrounds.

Each Theme is divided into two different sections: Video Transitions and Titles.

Themes with text can be customized, which means you can change the color, font, and look of the theme. The title Themes work as Connected Clips with the video elements positioned below the Connected Clip being integrated into the overall graphic.

139

Transition Themes work between clips and therefore there needs to be existing media on either side of the edit for the Transition to work.

Video and Audio Effects

There is a great selection of effects from which to draw. You can treat your images to create many different looks. Essentially all the effects, video or audio, work in a similar way.

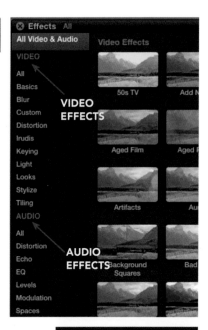

1   Click the Effects Browser icon (shortcut Command + 5). Look at the Effects Browser. There are separate headings for video and audio; click any of the headings to reveal the effects which are available, or choose All to see a complete listing of either video or audio effects.

2   You can preview any of the effects. Click to highlight the clip in the Timeline to which you wish to apply the effect; then position your curser over the effect in the Effects Browser and skim over it. The results will show in the Viewer.

Cross Hatch

Highlight a clip in the Timeline; select an effect and skim across to preview.

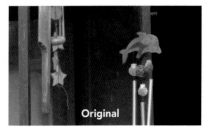

Original

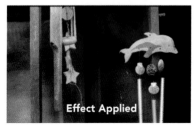

Effect Applied

3 With the clip highlighted in the Timeline, double-click the effect of choice. The effect will then be applied. Alternatively, drag the effect from the Effects Browser to a clip and the effect will then be applied. Play it back to view the result.

4 To adjust the effect parameters, select the clip in the Timeline to which the clip has been applied and then look towards the Inspector (Command + 4 to show Inspector).

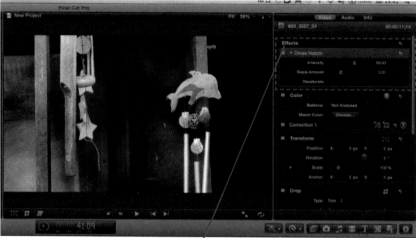

5 Under Video in the Inspector you will see Effects—here the choices to modify your effect are in front of you. You need to be aware that for prebuilt effects, the controls may be limiting. Regardless, there is still a lot that can be done. Experiment, get to know the options, and then you can put these effects to creative use when you need to add some sparkle to a production.

Note: You can easily switch the effect on and off in the Inspector by checking or unchecking the box next to the name of the effect. To delete the effect, click to highlight it in the Inspector and press the Delete key.

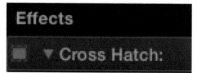

When working with audio effects, the procedure is the same: Highlight the clip, double-click the effect in the Effects Browser to apply, or use the drag and drop method.

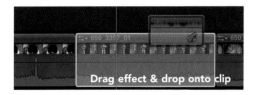

Drag effect & drop onto clip

Click the audio of a clip in the Timeline—go to the Inspector and reveal the audio controls. The audio effects are powerful and the results are played back in real time. Therefore, you can adjust video or audio parameters as you play to see or hear the result.

Effects			
■ ▼ AUHipass:			
	Preset:	Default ▼	
▼	Parameters:		
	cutoff frequency:	⚑	6900.0
	resonance:	⚑	0

Transitions

 Transitions are applied at the edit point between two clips. For a transition to work, you must have media to draw upon from each of the clips on the hard drive, beyond the media which has been edited into the Timeline. For example, for a 1-second transition to take place, you need half a second of extra media, for each clip, to be accessible on the drive beyond that you see in the Timeline.

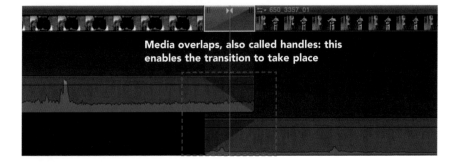

Media overlaps, also called handles: this enables the transition to take place

1 Press the Transitions Browser icon.

You can reveal all of the transitions or view the different categories.

2 Choose a transition and drag and drop. This positions the transition onto an edit point between two clips.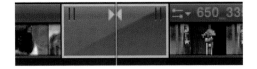

3 View the result. To change the duration, control-click and choose Change Duration.

Alternatively, click to highlight the transition and press Control + D, then enter the duration of choice into the Dashboard.

4 Select a transition in the Timeline. In the Inspector you have controls which will affect the look of the transition. Customize and play back to preview the results.

Note: When adding a dissolve, an audio dissolve will also be applied, if the video and audio are locked together as a single clip. If you have detached audio then a dissolve will only apply to the video.

143

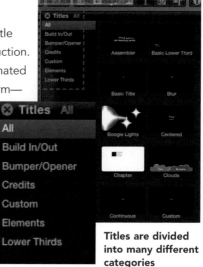

There are an amazing variety of transitions. Obviously, these need to be used with discretion, so the results are tasteful and appealing. Used well, these transitions can add shine to a production which otherwise may be visually static.

Text

Once upon a time, a simple title would suffice to open a production. These days, moving text, animated text, 3D text, and floating text are the norm— the demand for complex text creation is something that the editor is expected to deliver.

There is a wide variety of text options offered in Final Cut Pro X, ranging from a simple static title to moving text which can be customized in many different ways.

Titles are divided into many different categories

1 Select the Title icon in the Toolbar to reveal the Title Browser.

As with the other effects areas we have looked at so far, you can choose All to see the entire range, or there are separate categories to chose from.

2 Double-click any of the text options and this will be added as a Connected Clip wherever the Skimmer or Playhead is positioned. You can also choose to drag and drop the title from the Title Browser to the position of your choice.

3 In the Timeline, click the title and look to the Inspector. Press Command + 4 to bring the Inspector into view. Look to the top of the Inspector and there are two tabs: Title and Text. You enter text in the Text tab and change parameters in the Title tab.

Here, you can enter the text you wish to work with and adjust parameters such as font, size, spacing tracking, and alignment.

Basic		↰
Font: Helvetica ↕		Regular ↕
Size:	⬆	194.0
Alignment:	≣ ≣ ≣ ≣ ≣ ≣ ≣	
Vertical Alignment:	⊤ ± ⊥	
Line Spacing:	⬆	0
Tracking:	⬆	0 %
Kerning:	⬆	
Baseline:	⬆	0

4 Look to the Viewer. Assuming you have clicked the text in the Timeline, the Viewer will display the word "Title" superimposed over the background image.

5 Overtype the text information within the Viewer or in the Inspector window.

6 Adjust attributes of the text in the Inspector.

7 To reposition text, in the Viewer, click the icon on the far left, which is a square with circles on the edges in the bottom left of the Viewer

 window. This is referred to as the Transform Effect. With Transform Effect enabled you can reposition the text by dragging in the Viewer, resize the text by dragging the corners towards or away from the center, rotate the text by grabbing the handle in the center, and squeeze the text by choosing the point on the edges of the frame.

Note: The Transform Effect function is not just for titles, it can be used to manipulate video images as well. You can reposition, stretch images vertically or horizontally, and rotate.

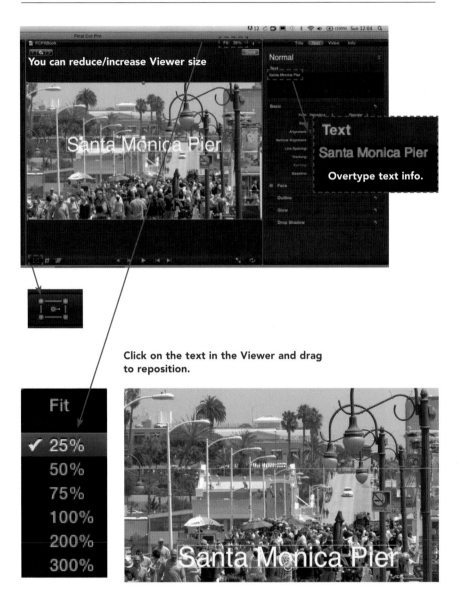

Click on the text in the Viewer and drag
to reposition.

Size the image using the percentage values. Choose Fit to make the image use
all of the available space, or you can enlarge or reduce the image. This is simply
a visual representation and does not affect the actual size of the image.

147

Drag corners to resize

Squeeze or stretch by moving center points

Grab center handle to rotate

Back in the days of film, this required an optical printer and tanks of chemicals to bring the image to life. Now we can make changes and play back in real time. This is a big deal!

  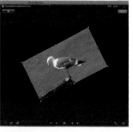

Increase/decrease size. **Stretch/squeeze the image.** **Rotate.**

Creating a Static Title

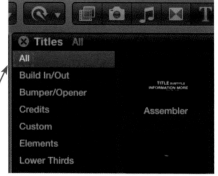

It is all well and good to have moving, animating, pulsating text, but sometimes you just want the words to sit on the screen, plain and simple.

1	In the Title Browser, select All to reveal all the text options.

2	Locate Custom; you can search for it at the bottom of the Text Browser or scroll down the list until you find it. Apply this to the Timeline by double-clicking or dragging.

3	In the Timeline, click the title, go to the Inspector, and enter the text details in the text area. Choose a font, size, and alignment.

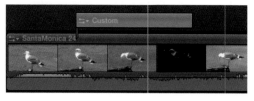

149

4   You can add color to the text. Check that
    Face is selected, choose the color, make
    a choice, and this will be reflected in the
    words that are on screen. You can also
    adjust the opacity and the blur.

5   You can also adjust outline, glow,
    and drop shadow.

Spend some time with text and you can customize
the appearance of the words to a high level.

ENGRAVERS MT
Euphemia UCAS
Eurostile
FLATBUSH
Footlight MT Light
Forgotten Futurist
Franklin Gothic Book
Franklin Gothic Medium
Futura
Garamond
✓ GAZ
GB18030   Bitmap
Geeza Pro
Geneva
Geneva CY
Georgia
Giddyup Std
Gill Sans
Gill Sans MT
Gill Sans Ultra Bold
Gloucester MT Extra Condensed
Goudy Old Style
Gujarati MT
Gulim
GungSeo
Gurmukhi MT
Haettenschweiler
Handwriting - Dakota
Harrington
HeadLineA
Hei

Note: When adjusting fonts you get a long list from which to choose. Each font is represented visually so you can gauge the appearance. If you scroll through the choice of fonts on screen, you will see the words changing so you know exactly how each font will appear.

Going Wacky with Fonts

Whenever you select a title, you have the option to radically change the appearance by drawing on a wide range of prebuilt options inside of Final Cut

Pro X. The choice is astounding, and the results are impressive. You can also customize the appearance in terms of font, color, and many other attributes.

1 Drop a title into the Timeline; double-click it, and look to the Inspector.

2 The top of the Inspector in the text area will read "Normal" in large letters. Choose the drop-down menu to reveal the range of choices.

3 Drag between the choices and choose one of the options. Click and release to see the result.

4 You can now customize the Face, Outline, Glow, and Drop Shadow options.

Fading Titles On and Off and Adjusting Transparency

To fade titles is a basic requirement and this can be achieved quite easily:

1   Choose Custom Title and apply it above a clip in the Timeline.

2   Click the title in the Timeline and refer to the Inspector. Type over the words.

3   Look at the title in the Timeline—to the left is a small drop-down arrow. Click this and choose Show Video Animation (shortcut Control + V).

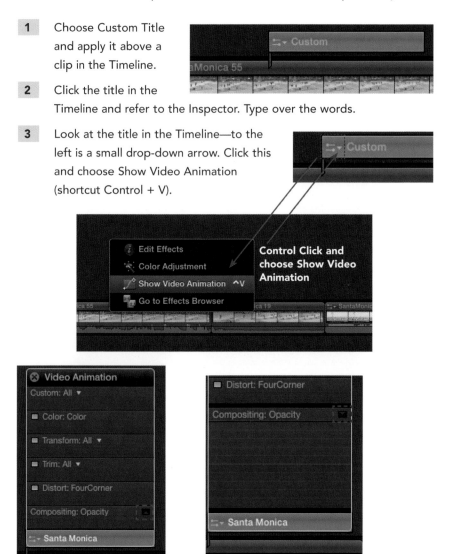

4   The Video Animation window will appear. Click the small arrow to the right of Compositing Opacity. This will open up the opacity controls.

5   Drag the ends to program a fade from the beginning and end. As you drag, you can see a numeric representation of the duration of the fade. You can also drag down the Opacity slider to make the words transparent. As you drag, a percentage read-out indicates the change in opacity.

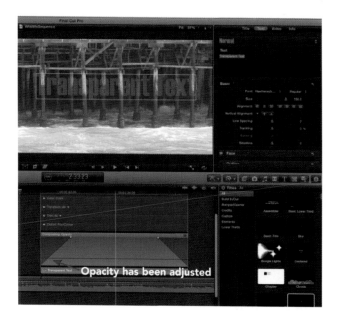

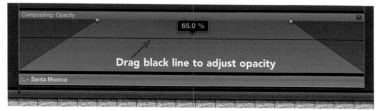

Below: You can see the text is transparent.

Keyframing Text

So you want to make your text move. You want it to start here and finish there.
You wish to program a move so that the text follows a particular path. This can
all be done in an elegant way with fine control by keyframing.

1   Place a title into the Timeline—I suggest using Custom Title.

2   Click the text in the Timeline, go to the Inspector or Viewer, and overtype the text as you require.

3   Using the settings in the
Inspector, adjust the font,
size, tracking, and any other
parameters you wish to
adjust. You can also adjust
the face and add a glow,
outline, or drop shadow.

4   In the Timeline, make sure the title is selected; at the bottom left of
the Viewer press the Transform Effect icon.

5 You can now freely position the text by dragging. Position and size the text.

6 Position the Playhead in the clip in the Timeline at the location you want the animation (move) to begin. Mark a Keyframe by pressing the Keyframe button at the top left of the Viewer interface.

7 Move forward in the Timeline to where you want the next Keyframe to be added. Reposition the text, rotate it, scale it, whatever you wish to do. This will automatically add the next Keyframe.

Keyframe 1.

Keyframe 2—note the red line indicating the path of the move.

To see your keyframes in the Timeline, click the title, click the small arrow to the left, select Video Animation, and look towards Transform All. Here you can see the keyframes have been plotted.

157

You can jump keyframe to keyframe and forward or backward using the arrows at the top left of the Viewer.

Keyframes can be repositioned by dragging.

8   Control-click the Keyframe points in Viewer and you can program the move to be smooth or linear.

9   You can choose to lock a point, which means it cannot be dragged, it is fixed.

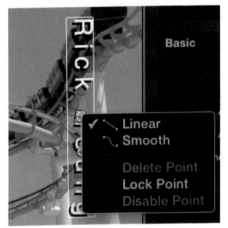

10 Option-click in the Keyframe editor to add further

points. You can add as many keyframes as you want.

This presents a visual way to get text to follow a particular path in a linear or smooth fashion. You can also Keyframe images using the same method. The procedure described is not exclusive to text.

Show Title/Action Safe Zones

When working with text, you need to pay attention to the safe area for titles.

When showing video content on a television, as opposed to a computer monitor, you will likely encounter what is known in the industry as cutoff, or the Essential Message Area (EMA). This means that not all of the image is seen on the television screen. As the editor of a program, we need to allow for this.

1   In the Viewer, choose the drop-down menu at the top right, scroll to the bottom, and switch on Show Title/Action Safe Zones.

2   Look to the Viewer. The outer lines represent Action Safe, while the inner lines represent Title Safe.

To ensure your titles are seen correctly off-air or on television monitors, position the words within the inside yellow lines.

For content that is not destined for broadcast or television viewing, you can disregard these safe areas; however, it is wise to adhere them, because if your content is shown on televisions then you know it will be safe.

DISPLAY
Show Video Scopes   ⌘7
Show Angle Viewer   ⇧⌘7
Show Both Fields

CHANNELS
✓ All
Alpha
Red
Green
Blue

OVERLAYS
✓ Show Title/Action Safe Zones

159

Generators

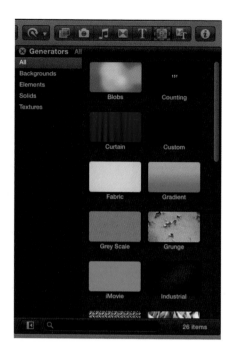

Generators provide prebuilt media inside of Final Cut Pro X. You can access the generators as a means of creating backgrounds, shapes, or texture to combine within your video compositions.

1   Click to reveal the Generators Browser.

2   You can choose to see all the generators which are available, or you can access the various categories.

3   Double-click a generator to add it to the Timeline and it will be inserted wherever the Skimmer or Playhead is positioned. Or you can drag and drop a generator, which can then be added to the Primary Storyline or as a Connected Clip.

Generator inserted into a Primary Storyline.

Generator as a Connected Clip.

If you drag a generator between clips it is inserted; if you drag it onto a clip you have the choice to perform a Replace edit.

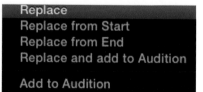

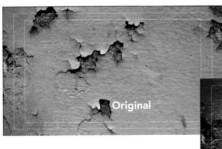

4 You can adjust the parameters of the generator in the Inspector and view changes in real time.

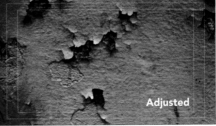

Note: Not all generators allow for adjustments.

Themes

Themes can be either titles or transitions. If a Theme is a title it works as a Connected Clip; if it is a transition then the theme is applied between two clips.

Themes combine graphical elements and text, and sometimes moving images. These are customizable but only to a point. You can change the text size and font, and, in some cases, you will choose moving images which will be integrated into the overall effect.

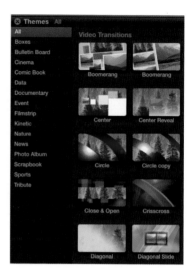

Working with Title Themes

1   Click to reveal the Themes Browser.

2   You can view all Themes or scan through the various categories.

3   Double-click one of the title Themes or drag into position and this will be added to the Timeline as a Connected Clip.

4   Double-click the title and you can enter text details in the Inspector, or you can type directly into the Viewer. You can also adjust size, font, tracking, and other details.

Other Themes involve prebuilt graphics which include video and text.

The text can be customized in terms of font choice, size, spacing, and color scheme; however, the overall look of the theme and the programmed animation moves cannot be changed.

Working with Transition Themes

As mentioned earlier, Themes can be worked with as either titles or transitions. To work with Transition Themes:

1 Click to reveal the Themes Browser.

2 Select one of the transition themes; these are clearly labeled as Video Transitions.

3 Drag the Video Transition to the edit point between two clips and this will then be applied.

4 Click the transition to reveal options in the Inspector which can be customized.

Colors can be manipulated and other attributes. These are prebuilt themes. As expected, the control

is limited; regardless, eye-catching results can be achieved by experimenting with the different settings.

5 To set the transition duration, control-click on the clip in the Timeline and choose Change Duration (shortcut Control + D).

Control + D and enter duration.

**Control-click
and select
Change Duration.**

Change Duration...   ^D
Expand Audio / Video   ^S
Show Precision Editor   ^E

It should be obvious that whichever of the Browsers you are working with, be it Effects, Transitions, Titles, Generators, or Themes, the process remains the same. You choose the effect, apply it, click to access controls in the Inspector, adjust, and then check out the result.

The wealth of effects in Final Cut Pro X is tremendous. When I started in television, the two-machine edit suite I was working with couldn't even do a dissolve—it was cuts only. To create a dissolve required separate tape sources to be run through a studio with vision mixer. Later a three-machine edit suite was purchased, which was referred to as the Super Suite. This could do dissolves and a few transitions but nothing like the results which Final Cut Pro X is capable of.

Transform Controls

This has already been discussed in-depth in relation to text - the same rules apply to video images when using the Transform Effect Controls. Any shot in the Timeline can be quickly repositioned, resized, rotated, and distorted. Furthermore, changes can be keyframed over time, meaning the image can be programmed to start in one position and end at another position.

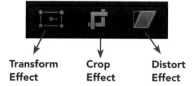

**Transform   Crop   Distort
Effect   Effect   Effect**

Look to the Viewer—at the bottom left are three buttons. These buttons represent Transform Effect, Crop Effect, and Distort Effect.

Transform

1   Click any clip in the Timeline.

2   Press the Transform Effect button. You will see overlay controls appearing in the Viewer.

3   Click the drop-down menu top right of the Viewer and set the size of the image so it is reduced onscreen.

Increase/decrease size.   **Stretch/squeeze the image.**   **Rotate.**

4   Drag from any of the corners to increase or decrease the image size.

5 Drag from the center points on the outside frame and you can squeeze or stretch the image.

6 Click the point attached to the center and you can then rotate the image. If you drag the center point outward, the circle increases in size and this will give you fine control when rotating.

Note: You can also access the Transform Controls in the video area of the Inspector.

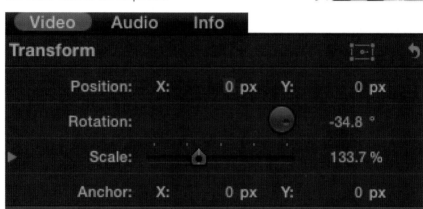

If you wish to Keyframe the video to move over time, the procedure is the same as described earlier in this chapter when keyframing text.

Crop Controls

There are three options offered within the crop controls: Trim, Crop, and Ken Burns.

Trim: To trim the image means to slice away either vertically or horizontally. If the image is positioned over another image, where the image is trimmed will reveal the image below.

Crop: Means to select a portion of the image and increase this in size to fill the frame. While sizing, the aspect ratio remains constant; therefore, the area you define is always the correct shape to fill the screen.

Ken Burns: This refers to pan and zoom controls. Named after American film director Ken Burns, who used the effect of panning and zooming across still images - the effect is known for creating moves across still images, but it can just as well be used for moving images.

Trimming Images

1 Highlight the clip in the Timeline.

2 Press Trim Top Left of the Viewer Interface.

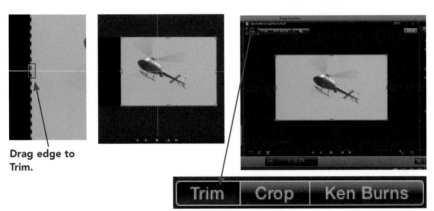

Drag edge to Trim.

3 Size the frame around the image by dragging or use the Crop controls in the Inspector.

4 Press done.

The result is the image shows exactly what you defined. When you trim an image in the Primary Storyline, then the result is black on-screen where you trimmed; if you trim a Connected Clip, where you have trimmed will be filled with the image below the Connected Clip, creating a picture-in-picture, or several picture-in-pictures if you are really creative.

You can also access controls in the Inspector.

You can also trim by numbers. Highlight the number in the Inspector and overtype, or use the arrow up/down keys for fine adjustment. You can then view subtle changes as you tap the keys.

To reset back to the default, go to the Crop controls in the Inspector and choose the arrow for reset or drop-down menu and select Reset Parameter.

Cropping Images

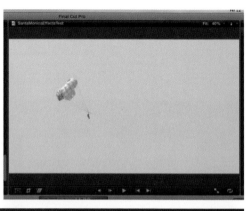

Adjusting crop is used to define an area of the image which will then fill the screen, whilst maintaining the original aspect ratio.

1 Highlight the clip you wish to crop in the Timeline.

2 Press the Crop Effect button on the lower left of the Viewer Interface.

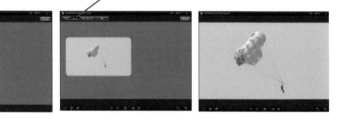

3 Click Crop on the top left.

4 Drag to set the crop size or use the crop controls in the Inspector. You will notice that you are constrained to the aspect ratio of the video you are working with. You can then position, by dragging, the crop area over the image.

5 Press done. The result will be before you—the area you defined now fills the screen. Beware of a loss of quality by cropping as, essentially, you are blowing up the image, or, more precisely, cropping in on the image.

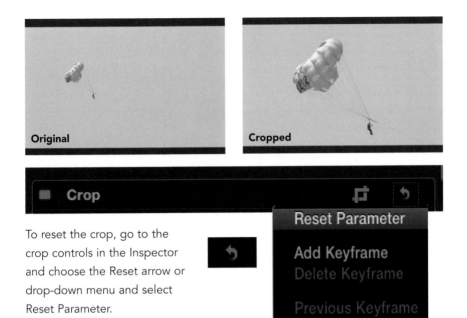

Original

Cropped

To reset the crop, go to the crop controls in the Inspector and choose the Reset arrow or drop-down menu and select Reset Parameter.

Crop

Reset Parameter

Add Keyframe

Delete Keyframe

Previous Keyframe

Next Keyframe

Working with the Ken Burns Effect

Ken Burns is an American documentarian who made extensive use of panning and zooming over still images. This technique has become associated with his name, though the technique itself predates Ken Burns' use of it. The effect can be used for still or moving images.

To work with the Ken Burns effect:

1 Click to select a clip in the Timeline.

2 Click the Crop button in the lower left of the Viewer.

3 At the top left-click Ken Burns.

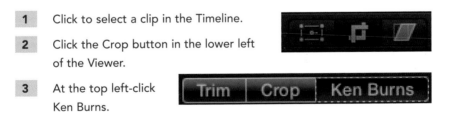

4   Your image will now appear with a green box and a red box—each of these is used to set the start (green) and end (red) points.

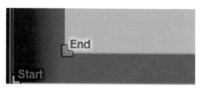

5   Drag the edges of the green box to define the start point of the move. If

you want all of the image, leave the green set to the outer edges of the image; if you wish to start already zoomed in to a portion of the image, then frame accordingly with the green box.

6 Drag the red box and size this to define the end of the move. If the red box is smaller than the green box, then you will zoom in to the image. If the red box is larger than the green box, the

result will be a zoom out. Be aware you can also use the crop controls in the Inspector to make adjustments. While adjusting, the aspect ratio will be restricted to that of the frame you are working with.

7 Press the Done button and press Play to check the result.

You can program beautiful slow zooms or rapid moves in on a portion of the image. Beware with the Ken Burns effect in Final Cut Pro X that the start point is always the beginning of the shot and the end point is the end of the shot. Therefore, if you need greater control, such as having a static image to begin with and then zoom in to, then manual keyframing would be needed to achieve the result.

Note: You can reverse the start and end points and reverse the direction of the effect. The second button is to play the effect.

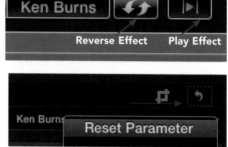

To reset at any stage, go to the crop controls in the Inspector and choose the arrow for the reset or drop-down menu and select Reset Parameter.

Distort Controls

Back in the early 1990s, I was watching a demo at a tradeshow on a high-end paint system. The operator was demonstrating a technique known as corner pinning—a digital still was positioned and stretched by dragging each of the four corners. This ability is right there in Final Cut Pro X for you to access.

1   Highlight a clip in the Timeline.

2   Press Distort.

3   Drag the corners and position as you wish. You can choose to crop the image and then distort as you wish.

Using the distort controls enables you to reshape the image by dragging each of the corners.

Above: Two layers composited together with the positioning of the sign done with the distort controls. A tint has been applied to the image on the left.

4   In the Distort Controls
of the Inspector, you
can key in numbers
manually or highlight
the numbers and use
the arrows to increase
or decrease the value.

Distort					
Bottom Left:	X:	568.1 px	Y:	194.6 px
Bottom Right:	X:	-78.4 px	Y:	176.8 px
Top Right:	X:	-43.7 px	Y:	13.0 px
Top Left:	X:	572.2 px	Y:	30.8 px

The controls for Transform, Crop, and Distort as found at the bottom left of the
viewer are also mirrored in the Inspector. Here, you can manually drag sliders or
enter numeric values.
If you enter numeric
values, highlight the
number and use the
up/down arrows for subtle changes.

Transform   Crop   Distort

Video	Audio	Info

SantaMonica 54   00:00:16;20

Transform

Position:	X:	-100.0 px	Y:	-8.0 px
Rotation:				1.7 °
Scale:				159 %
Anchor:	X:	0 px	Y:	0 px

Crop

Type:	Trim
Left:	480.0 px
Right:	213.6 px
Top:	203.6 px
Bottom:	0 px

Distort

Bottom Left:	X:	562.1 px	Y:	194.6 px
Bottom Right:	X:	-78.4 px	Y:	176.8 px

If you control-click in the Viewer you can choose:

Transform: Shift + T

Crop: Shift + C

Distort: Shift + D

Transform ⇧T
Crop ⇧C
Distort ⇧⌘D
None

Basic Keyframing

Keyframing has already been mentioned several times. It means to change over time.

You can Keyframe text, shapes, and moving images. You can also Keyframe the crop controls such as Transform, Crop, and Distort.

So far we have already covered keyframing text and keyframing audio. Let's run through the process for keyframing video:

1 Highlight a clip in the Timeline.

2 Click the Transform Effect button in the lower left of the Viewer.

3 Position the Playhead in the Timeline on the clip where you want the change to start. Resize and position the clip in the Viewer.

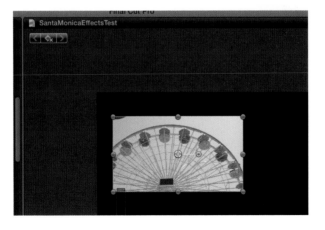

4 Click the Add Keyframe button; this will be your start Keyframe.

5 Move the Scrubber Bar forward in the Timeline.

6 Drag to adjust the size or positioning of the image. The next Keyframe will be marked automatically when you reposition the shot.

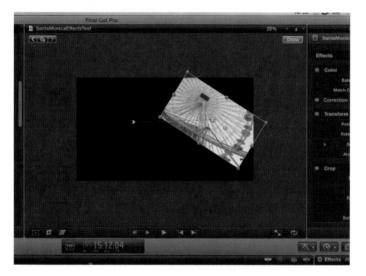

7 You may choose to position the clip you are Keyframing over a second layer of video (below). Therefore, the two images are composited together.

8 Playback and check the result. If you open the video animation controls and look to Transform All you can then see the Keyframes plotted. These can be dragged to extend or reduce the duration of the effect and further Keyframes can be added by pressing Option + Click in Transform All.

Show Video Animation ^V

Click the arrow above and choose Show Video Animation.

Open video animation and you can see the Keyframes plotted in the Transform All area.

Click to drag the Keyframes.

Option Click in Transform All to add further Keyframes.

179

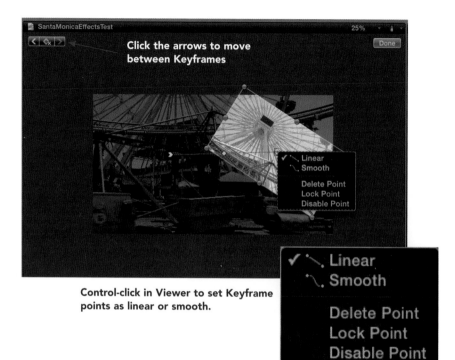

Control-click in Viewer to set Keyframe points as linear or smooth.

Stabilization

Built into Final Cut Pro X is the ability to add stabilization to any clip. This will remove minor shakes and can improve the usability of footage.

Simply click the clip in the Timeline, look to the Inspector, and switch on Stabilization (blue).

Wait while your footage is analyzed or continue working and come back once the process is complete.

Stabilization works well with the preset values; of course, change and tweak these to your own needs.

Keying

There are two types of keying available, both found in the
Effects Browser of Final Cut Pro X. If you search for "key"
both keyers will be found.

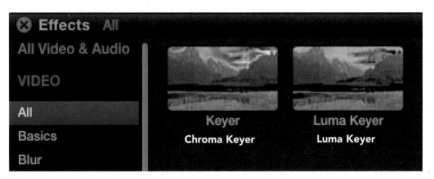

Chroma Key

Chroma key works on the amount of color information in the image. Often
referred to as blue screen or green screen, a chroma key will be built from two
layers: a background and a keying source. This enables you to key a person, on
one layer, over a background on a separate layer.

The chroma keyer in Final Cut Pro X is what I refer to as a three-click chroma keyer.

 1   Drop the Keyer on the clip in the Timeline.

2   Set key to matte.

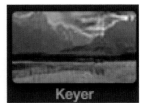

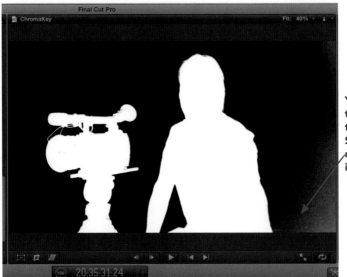

You can see the key is less than perfect. Spill to the right of screen is visible.

3   Refine the key. Go to the Inspector and choose Sample Color. This lets you draw a box over the troublesome area.

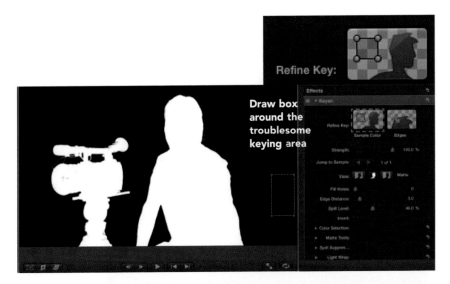

Refine Key:

Draw box
around the
troublesome
keying area

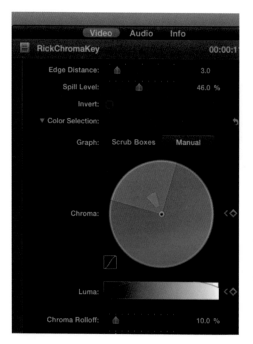

The result is an excellent key, depending on how well shot the camera original is.

You can tweak other settings within the Inspector. From my experience, as long as your original material is well shot and lit you will have no trouble in getting a good key out of Final Cut Pro X.

Having worked with many keyers for over 20 years in this business I can truly say the keyer included with Final Cut Pro X is certainly one of the best, if not the best, keyer on the market.

Luma Key

Luma key is different than chroma key. It works on the amount of luminance in an image, or the difference between black and white. Luma key used to be

used in television stations to key white word graphics filmed off black card by a live camera over another live source. This example is primitive by today's standards, but shows the history of this technique. Today, luma key is used in effects production and image composition.

Luma keys work particularly well with images that have a lot of contrast or separation of black and white. Look to the image on the previous page. The wire is exclusively black and the other parts of the image are much lighter. This is the sort of image which will key well.

1   Position the two clips in the Timeline with the image to key above the image which is to be the background image.

2   Apply the luma key to the video source.

3   Select matte so you can check the key level.

Effects

■ ▼ Luma Keyer:

Luma:

Invert: ☑

Luma Rolloff: ♠ . . . . 0 %

185

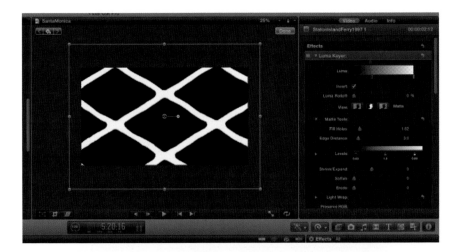

4   In the Inspector tweak the key using the luma controls. You can invert the source if you wish.

5   Adjust the controls to clean up the key as much as possible.

6   Switch the matte off to view the keyed result and adjust controls in the Inspector as necessary.

Quite effective results can be achieved by luma keying. The technique is useful for different types of effect production and provides a way to manipulate and composite images.

I've used many luma keyers and, like the chroma keyer, the luma keyer in Final Cut Pro X is definitely one of the best.

Color Correction

The color correction tools included Final Cut Pro X enable you to achieve results quickly so you can check out a variety of different looks. You can draw on different presets, and you can use dedicated controls to adjust the color, saturation, and exposure of an image. You can also choose to auto-color correct, though this is something which I tend to avoid!

Check the Balance option and Final Cut Pro X will auto-balance the color for you. As mentioned, I avoid this, as I believe the best results come from manual color correction. Regardless, for a very quick grade, auto-balance is an option.

Above: Original.

Above: Auto-balanced.

Now, let's move on to manual color correction.

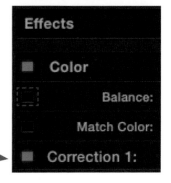

1 Highlight a clip in the Timeline.

2 Look to the Inspector to the color controls. Make sure auto-balance is switched off.

3 Check color correction is switched on (blue).

4 Press the arrow to the right of the Correction option and this will reveal three areas for color adjustment: color, saturation, and exposure.

189

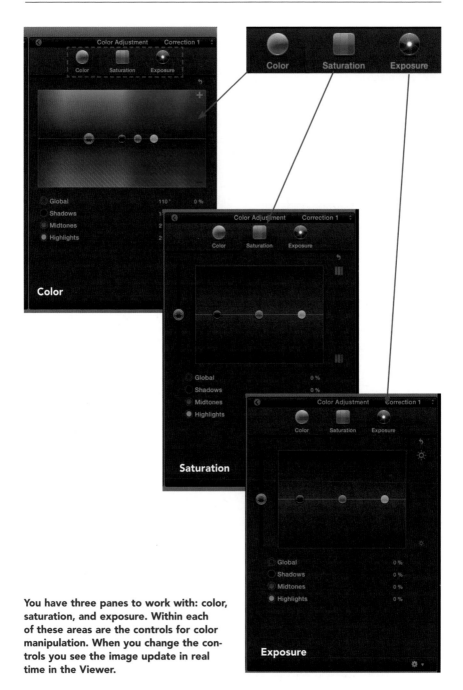

You have three panes to work with: color, saturation, and exposure. Within each of these areas are the controls for color manipulation. When you change the controls you see the image update in real time in the Viewer.

Color Board

The Color Board is where that you make adjustments to the color of the image. You can adjust the color globally, which means change the color across the entire image, or you can choose to be selective about which parts of the image are affected, by choosing to adjust the shadows, midtones, and highlights.

Each of the colors on the Color Board is controlled by the buttons

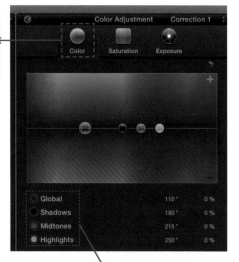

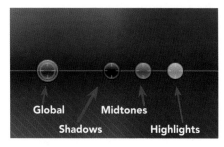

to the left. You choose a button to adjust the image globally, or to target the shadows, midtones, or highlights.

When color correcting, it can be very useful to turn on the video scopes where you can see a waveform monitor or vectorscope display of the image.

Choose the Window menu and scroll down to Show Video Scopes.

The Viewer will now split into two areas: (1) the video scopes and (2) the image you are viewing.

You can quickly toggle the scopes on off by pressing Command +7.

Window	Help	
Minimize		⌘M
Minimize All		
Zoom		
Go to Event Browser		⌘1
Go to Viewer		⌘3
Go to Timeline		⌘2
Go to Inspector		⌥⌘4
Go to Color Board		⌘6
Go to Audio Enhancements		⌘8
Show Project Library		⌘0
Hide Event Library		⇧⌘1
Show Timeline Index		⇧⌘2
Show Inspector		⌘4
Show Video Scopes		⌘7

The scopes update in real time as the video plays and you can choose to show a histogram, waveform monitor, or vectorscope.

Click settings and choose how you want to view the scopes.

These are professional tools designed to monitor the video signal for broadcast output. If the destination of the content you are producing is for broadcast television, then the scopes are very important. If the content you are producing is to be viewed on computers, home systems, or the web, then you don't need to adhere to broadcast standards.

Regardless, this provides a scientific way to monitor the video signal for those who need to do this.

Working with the Color Board

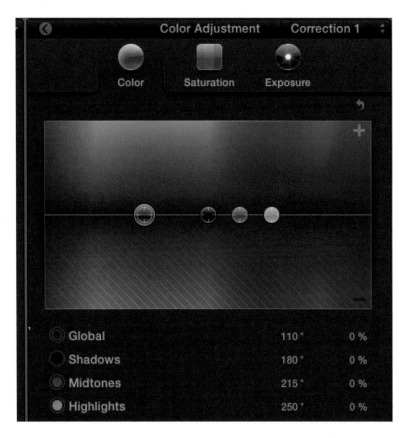

The main job of the Color Board is to enable you to adjust color either globally, meaning throughout the entire image, or to limit the color adjustments to the shadows, midtones, or highlight parts of the image.

To adjust the overall color of the image click on the global control and drag it to different parts of Color Board. The original image is then altered by the color adjustment you make. If you push to the top of the Color Board, the amount of color is increased; if you drop below the middle line and drag in the opposite direction, the amount of color is decreased.

Note: Instead of dragging a control, you can use the up or down arrows on the keyboard for fine adjustment. This also works while video is playing.

The positioning on the color board of the global control directly influences the look of the shot.

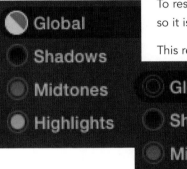

To reset to the original, press the Global button so it is highlighted, then press the Delete key. This returns the image to its original state.

Working with the separate buttons for shadows, midtones, and highlights lets you adjust the color for each of these areas. Remember, use the up/down arrows

for fine control. This works even while the image plays.

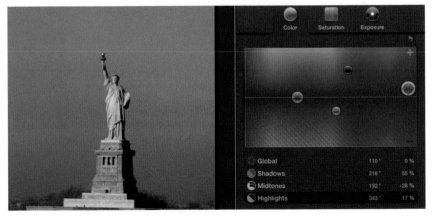

Adjusting Saturation

The process is very similar to that described for working with the Color Board.
A master global slider is accessible on the left, with independent controls for
shadows, midtones, and highlights.

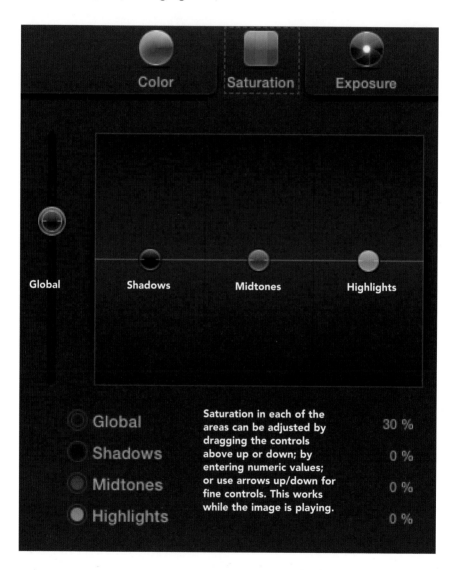

Controls at defaults

Originals

Saturation boosted

Adjust Global, Shadows, Midtones, Highlights

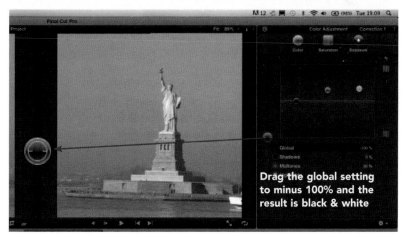

Drag the global setting to minus 100% and the result is black & white

197

Exposure Adjustment

Changing the exposure is an effective tool in bringing out the best in an image. The obvious use is to correct under- or overexposed images, and this is a valid use. However, it is not all about getting an image technically correct, it is also about getting what works best, the result you want to achieve. The look of an image can be considerably improved by tweaking the exposure.

The Exposure tools work the same as the process described when adjusting Saturation.

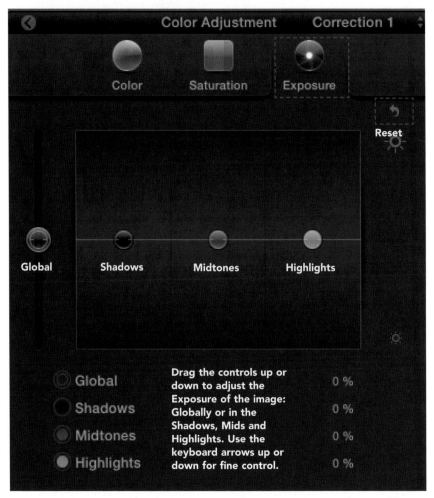

Controls at defaults

Original

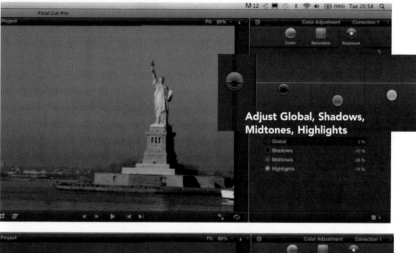

Adjust Global, Shadows, Midtones, Highlights

Drag down for darker and up to lighten the image.

Color Presets

At the bottom right of each window in Color Adjustment is a gear icon which lets you switch between color presets.

Click this and a list will be revealed. These are color presets which can applied to your image. It is as simple as choosing a preset, applying it, and checking out the result.

Save Preset...

Alien Lab
Artificial Light
Ash
Brighten
Cold CCD
Contrast
Cool
Dew
Dim
Dry
Dust
Fall Sun
Frost
Moonlight
Night
Sewer
Spring Sun
Summer Sun
Warm
Winter Sun

Once you have applied the preset you can then go into each of the areas: color, saturation, and exposure and change the parameters.

Regardless of which areas you are working in you can reset to defaults by pressing the reset button.

You can also highlight any of the numeric values and press Delete to reset that particular value. This is advantageous over the Reset button which resets all the parameters within a particular area. Think of the Reset button as being a global reset and highlighting the numbers and pressing Delete as being a more targeted or focused way of doing it.

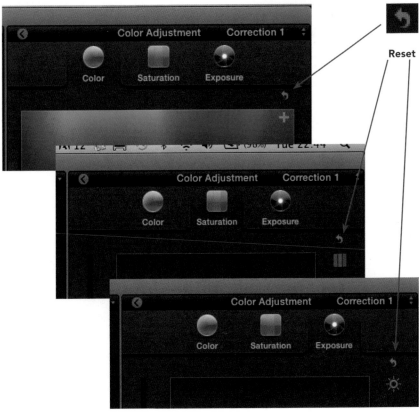

Reset

Once you have manually adjusted settings, you can save this as a preset:

1 Click the gear icon bottom right of the Inspector and choose Save Preset.

2 Name the preset. This will now appear at the bottom of the Preset List.

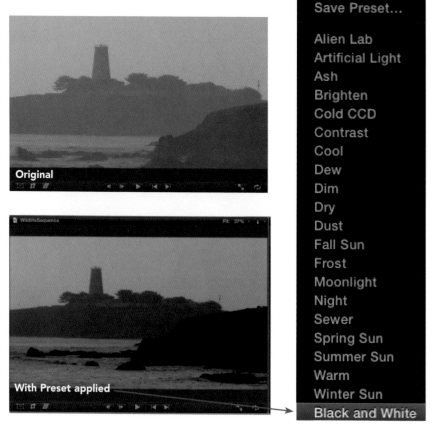

You can also copy and paste effects:

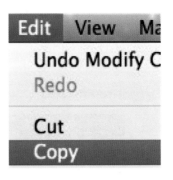

1 Highlight the clip in the Timeline, which has already been color corrected or has an effect already applied to it.

2 Press Command + C to copy or select from the Edit menu.

3 Select another clip or clips in the Timeline.

4 Chose Paste Effects from the Edit menu or type Command + Option + V.

Note: This will then apply all effects that are applied to the original clip.

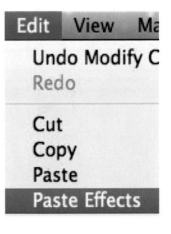

Share   Window   Help

Media Browser...
Apple Devices...
DVD...
Blu-ray...

Email...

YouTube...
Facebook...
Vimeo...
CNN iReport...

SHARE

Export Media...   ⌘E
Save Current Frame...
Export Image Sequence...
Export for HTTP Live Streaming...

Send to Compressor...
Export Using Compressor Settings...

Export Media Using Share

When you have finished your movie, the time has come for output. Using the Share facility in Final Cut Pro X you can output for a master file, produce a DVD, Blu-ray, or upload direct to YouTube, Facebook, Vimeo, or CNN iReport. Share is the final part of the process and enables you to get your edit in front of its intended audience.

By far the most important part of Share for the professional editor is the means to create a master file. Using the Export Media option, you can choose to produce a file with the same properties as the project—Current Settings—or there are other output settings to choose from.

All the Apple ProRes options are available plus you can also encode to H.264, Uncompressed 8- or 10-bit 4:2:2, DVCPro HD, and XDCAM. The Current Settings option for output is used to create a master file which exactly matches your project settings.

1 Go to the Project Library and highlight the project you wish to export.

Highlight the project in the Project Library.

Properties   Sharing

SantaMonica   00:18:02;02
Default Event: SantaMonica   1080p HD
1920x1080 | 29.97p   Stereo | 48kHz

2 Look to the Inspector. This will show you the Project Properties as they are currently set. This will define the output codec when using Current Settings in Share.

3 If you wish to change the properties of the project, click the wrench icon at the bottom right of the Inspector. A window will open giving you a choice of many parameters. You can choose the format, resolution, and codec. The settings defined here define the output of the project when using Current Settings in Share.

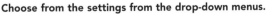

Choose from the settings from the drop-down menus.

4 Choose the Share menu and scroll to Export Media (shortcut **Command + E**).

Share **Window** **Help**

Export Media... **⌘E**

5 You can choose to export video and audio, video only, or audio only.

✓ **Video and Audio**

Video Only

Audio Only

6 Leave the video codec at Current Settings.

Export "SantaMonica"

Options   Summary

Export: Video and Audio

Video codec: Current Settings

7 Save to a file to a location of your choice.

Save As: SantaMonicaEdit

Desktop

Once the output is complete you will have a master QuickTime file, in the codec the project is set to.

You can also choose to export using
the different codecs that are offered:

1 Highlight a project in the Project Library.

2 Choose the Share menu.

3 Scroll to Export Media.

Share | Window | Help

Media Browser...
Apple Devices...
DVD...
Blu-ray...

Email...

YouTube...
Facebook...
Vimeo...
CNN iReport...

Export Media...

Current Settings

Apple ProRes 4444
Apple ProRes 422 (HQ)
✓ Apple ProRes 422
Apple ProRes 422 (LT)
Apple ProRes 422 (Proxy)
H.264
Uncompressed 8–bit 4:2:2
Uncompressed 10–bit 4:2:2

DVCPRO HD
HDV / XDCAM HD (25 Mbps)
XDCAM EX (35 Mbps)
XDCAM HD (35 Mbps)
XDCAM HD422 (50 Mbps)

Export
Video codec
Audio file format
Open with

4 Select Export and choose the codec you wish to export to. You can choose the four levels of ProRes, H.264, Uncompressed 8-bit or 10-bit 4:2:2, DVCPro HD, HDV, XDCAM EX/HD.

5 Define where you want the file to be saved. The result will be a QuickTime file in the codec you have chosen.

Save As: SantaMonicaEdit

Desktop

▼ DEVICES
Rick Young's MacBook Pro (3)
iDisk
Macintosh HD
Untitled
Thunderbolt1
▼ PLACES
Desktop

24HourMovies
28 – 80mm tests.mov
50mmF1.2.mov
80 – 200mm.mov
80-200mm
180Tests
180Tests.mov
501.2
650_159...1 (id).mov

You can use the Share facility to export to Apple devices, meaning iPad, iPhone, and iPod.

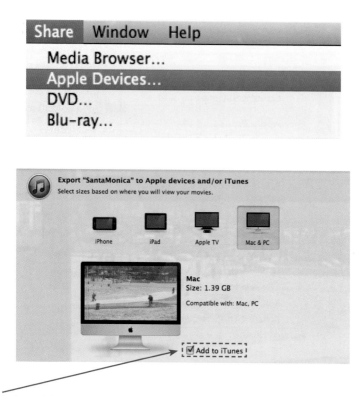

Check the Add to iTunes button if you wish for the file to be added to your iTunes library once encoding has finished.

You then define if the file is to be compatible with both Mac and PC; or if the encode is for iPhone, iPad, or Apple TV.

Of particular use to video editors is the ability to quickly and easy knock out a DVD or a Blu-ray of an edit.

Simply choose DVD or Blu-ray from the Share menu and you can then set various parameters to customize the disc.

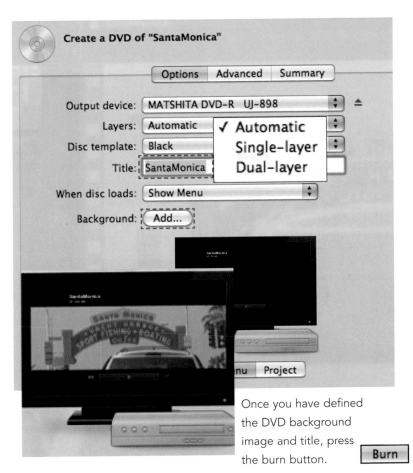

Once you have defined the DVD background image and title, press the burn button.

Likewise, you can also produce a Blu-ray disc. The process is similar to producing a DVD; however, there are some extra options such as the ability to add a logo graphic along with the title graphic. For both DVD and Blu-ray, you can choose whether the disc loads to a menu or the movie plays straight away.

Share	Wind
Media Brow	
Apple Devi	
DVD...	
Blu-ray...	

✓ Show Menu
Play Movie

Final Cut Pro

Create a Blu-ray disc of "SantaMonica"

Options   Advanced   Summary

Output device: MATSHITA DVD-R UJ-898 (AVCHD) ⬆

Layers: Automatic

Disc template: Black

Title: SantaMonica

When disc loads: Show Menu

☐ Include loop movie button

Background: Add...

Logo graphic: Add...

Title graphic: Add...

✓ Show Menu
Play Movie

Main Menu   Project

Cancel

The authoring is basic but effective. This isn't designed to be a full-blown DVD or Blu-ray authoring system, but it does provide an easy means to produce

DVDs or Blu-ray discs for client viewing or a quick hard copy of the edit ready to view at home.

| Share | Window | Help |

Media Browser...
Apple Devices...
DVD...
Blu-ray...

Email...

YouTube...
Facebook...
Vimeo...
CNN iReport...

Export Media...
Save Current Frame...
Export Image Sequence...
Export for HTTP Live Streaming...

Send to Compressor...
Export Using Compressor Settings

For those who use Compressor, Apple's encoding application, you can send a file directly to Compressor from Final Cut Pro X.

On choosing this command, Compressor will then open and you can apply and tweak the encoding setting within this application.

My preferred method is to create a master file, as described earlier, and to then encode from the master.

Once you have a master file you are happy with, back it up on several hard drives. This is the equivalent of a negative from the days of film. A pure digital copy of the edit is produced in Final Cut Pro X. You may then choose to copy the associated media to a separate hard drive just so you know everything is protected and intact for the moment you need to access it.

ProRes
4 Settings

Uncompressed
2 Settings

Video Sharing Services
5 Settings

HD 1080p Video Sharing
HD 1080p for upload to web sharing sites such as YouTube and Vimeo.

Apple ▸ Apple Devices ▸ 1080p for Apple Devices (10 Mbps)

Above: You can also use Export Using Compressor Settings which means you access the Compressor Settings directly within Final Cut Pro X.

213

Final Cut Pro X is now becoming established as a viable editor in the professional world of post production. The program is making great strides forward with every update, and the pace of development is speeding along.

Since the initial release in June 2011, there have been five updates within a single year. It is clear that Apple is working hard to build this into a serious tool that is used at many levels.

We're living in a digital age in which the moving image and the ability to create moving images are now as common as the still image. Just about everyone has a video camera of some sort, whether it is in a camera phone, a dedicated video camera, or some other device. Video literacy is the foundation of mass media in the twenty-first century, and being literate in producing edited content is found from schoolchildren to high-end professional editors.

Whether you edit at the professional level or for other reasons, Final Cut Pro X provides the means to produce content exceptionally quickly with top-level results. The tools are there to draw on, it depends how good you are, as the editor, to pull it all together and really make it work.

I started editing on a Mac way back in 1998. Before then I was working in tape suites. I've been exposed to many systems from film editing to multi-machine tape editing, the original Final Cut Pro and many other computer-based editing systems.

Final Cut Pro X is different. The approach is different. Apple has deliberately shredded the old model and built something new. The benefits are clear if you can absorb this way of working and refine it to your own needs.

In this book, I have outlined many work methods I use to get results using Final Cut Pro X. I'm a professional editor; I produce content daily and weekly for paying clients. I use Final Cut Pro X because it works for me, and more importantly, it produces results my clients are happy with.

When Final Cut Pro X was released in June 2011, amid a firestorm of controversy, I said to someone at the time: "Can it do a cut? Can it do a dissolve? Can it separate audio from video?" The answer was obviously yes! "So what's the problem?" was my reply.

That's it! Go and edit. The way to learn Final Cut Pro X is to use it. The tool is good, now make it work for you so you hit the mark, dead center, bull's eye, every time.

Index